AF893789

Magnus Hellman

How Attractive Employers succeed

The Leadership That Makes Us Productive and Committed

INUBI Publishing

© Magnus Hellman and INUBI Publishing
Helsingborg 2019

ISBN: 978-91-985710-0-4

TABLE OF CONTENTS

INTRODUCTION

The workplace is a dynamic, ever-changing entity. Standards in a company environment in earlier years are no longer acceptable. In the corporate world, companies are faced with mounting changes in technology and the workforce itself. Any CEOs and company leaders who wish to maintain a competitive edge and see their enterprises succeed and thrive, need to take note of changes in society and the types of work environment they provide for their staff.

Whereas in the past, the way to grow a company may have focused more on the product or service offered, corporations today see the need to attract and keep the very best talent available in their markets. This is because the quality of service to customers and clients has become as important --- if not more critical--- than the pricing of products or the innovation of services provided.

This book aims to look at a various of factors that go into creating a dynamic and positive work environment for the benefit of company leaders who want to stay ahead of the curve in their respective fields. We will make the case in the chapters that nothing can more ensure the growth and vitality of a company than a prominent focus on the attraction and acquisition of the best talent available. And then, when having the talent on board, how to keep them with the company and set up an environment where people become the most reliable asset of the company.

We will be examining the culture of a company and why it is essential to the overall vitality of a positive and successful culture, and how to achieve that environment. We will demonstrate that the company can use that culture as part of its branding. In the end, the most important thing for any employer is the way people speak and feel about the organization.

A vibrant workforce is the most valuable asset a company can have in these competitive financial times, so knowing what kind of talent a company should be looking for needs to be highlighted, as well as how to conduct fruitful searches for the best talent. Some companies view the onboarding process as a period of quick training and indoctrination in the company and the first positions the new hires will work in. But we try to show that a robust onboarding process is crucial to employee morale and building up the company culture.

In these modern times with big changes in the labor market, we will take a detailed look at what is called the gig workers as a part of the gig economy --- using freelancers as part of the workforce --- and the considerations that a company must make in the 21st Century to take this vast pool of talent into account. We need to examine the pros and cons of employers drawing talent from the gig economy pool.

The benefit packages will have its natural place in the book --- what they are and the importance they have in a company's ability to attract and keep the best employees. By looking at the benefits that employees find most attractive and desirable, leaders will be in a better position to put together benefit packages that best serve the needs of the company and its workforce.

There have been some new ways recently developed of increasing motivation at the workplace. One of these is gamification. Gamification? Yes, we will define and describe the theory, what beneficial effects it can have and how to implement gamification into the tasks and procedures of the company.

We are all human beings with a life outside the work. Some of us think it´s important to have a rich social life and others do not. No matter what our private life means to us individually, we need to discuss the considerable importance of a healthy work/life balance. We demonstrate that the old "nose to the grindstone" mentality of prioritizing work above all else --- including employees' private home lives --- is no longer sustainable. So, if leaders wish to reduce stress and increase worker morale while avoiding high staff turnover, leadership must make a healthy balance between work responsibilities and the private lives of their employees a core issue. We also need to look at the topic of trust in the workplace and its existence as a primary factor in productivity and job satisfaction. We will argue for the benefits that companies can accrue by building trust amongst managers and staff. Still, it takes a willingness on the part of leadership to give some control away to their employees and to learn the value of open communication and a spirit of collaboration.

As a link to leadership, we will examine the idea that modern leadership is more about coaching. We will go into some detail about the difference between old-school management styles and leaders acting as coaches for their staff, and how coaching others leads to building good leaders in the employee ranks. This will lead directly to the concept of employee co-leading. Because of the other mindsets and work models discussed, we try to show that employers who implement the ideas presented previously will be able to transition into a place of shared leadership between management and staff. While we believe that co-leading warrants thorough consideration for the future, we will honestly look at the disadvantages of co-leading, along with the many positives that can happen in such a work model.

At last, we will examine the factors that go into creating a work environment for the 21st Century that will be most likely to bring about growth and value, and help those in leadership to put all the pieces together to ensure that their companies are positioned to grow and produce well into the future.

CHAPTER ONE

The Importance of a Healthy Company Culture

Just as each country has a culture that reflects the general way of life of its people, companies also have their own unique cultures. Company culture transcends a company's simple business practices to the behavior, values, and attributes that define how it operates. An engaging company culture attracts the best workers around toward that company, as well as helping to retain and motivate existing employees to be at their best. The culture showcases the workplace values, the style and identity of the company, and the attitude that drives the company. Positive company culture gives satisfaction to employees, making them look forward to each workday.

The culture is the tool that drives the company image and keeps people talking about the brand. It is so significant that no aspect of the business is left untouched by it. It involves everything from recruitment, employee satisfaction, customer relations and many other needs in the company. Effective company culture is such that values the workforce, so that they are happy being a part of the company and look forward to their time at the workplace.

Is company culture that important? A recent study by Deloitte --- the world's largest professional services network --- bears this out. The study showed that 88% of employees and 94% of company executives believe strongly that business success is reliant on a distinct corporate company culture.[1] The survey further highlighted that employees who are valued at the workplace and are happy with their job are most prevalent in companies have a positive and strong culture.

Healthy cultures, therefore, should be the backbone of those companies striving to be rated as the best organizations to work for among the workforce. Such organizations that have a positive and strong corporate culture working for them will attain high status within their industry, motivating employees to work most conscientiously and productively for themselves and the good of the company.

A vibrant company culture revolves around the mission, vision, and values that are unique to that organization --- NOT the product. The difference between powerhouse brands that are renowned for their performance is in WHY they do what they do, as their most prioritized value. Simon Sinek, a leadership expert who is very passionate about healthy company culture states that companies with a weak culture focus first on WHAT (the product) rather than the WHY (the unique vision) of their company.

Sinek explains this in what he calls the Golden Circle illustration. It is common to find many company leaders starting with the WHAT and HOW of their product to make sales, only explaining the WHY they do what they do as low in company priority. In contrast, Simon Sinek believes great brands and leaders go the opposite way by emphasizing and explaining the WHY behind their company as the topmost priority. It impacts on all decision making in the company and drives the company culture in a positive direction.

In a similar survey by CultureIQ, a 20% higher satisfaction rating is given by employees whose companies have a strong culture in terms of the companies' focus on values, the collaboration between individuals and departments, and overall work environment.

Challenges on the Way of Building a Company Culture

Many challenges stand in the way of company leaders when building a culture in a specified direction. These challenges are diverse. Sometimes they can come from the management in terms of policies, goals, and resources available. On the other hand, challenges can come from the nature of employees in the company. Here are some core challenges

Unhappy and Discouraged Employees

Discovering the mindset of the employees and finding out that they are not at all as motivated and excited as the company would desire, can be one major hurdle to cross if instilling a new company culture. The employer can hardly make any substantial changes when the employees are bored and unhappy in their current position in the establishment. This is about the major challenge top leaders identify in the culture development process. The employer must first listen to their employees and see ways to build trust back to the company.

The Generational Gap

We live in very fast-paced times. Companies may have older staff who have worked with them for decades. But in today's jet age, Millennials have a very different outlook on the world around them which carries over to the work environment.

Human Resources (HR) personnel face this difficulty surrounding diverse generational workforce daily. Bridging the gap between the older worker and Millennials and Gen X can be a daunting challenge to build a great company culture.

According to Charles Ashworth, an expert on employee success, as most companies recruit more millennials into their workforce, it tends to create a demographic of diverse digital orientation.[2] It's then the job of company leaders to accommodate this diversity in familiarity and compatibility of the use of technology. The proverbial generation gap hence stands in the way of building a strong culture in this regard. The fact is though, that companies should rather see the good in diversity, leveraging the generations' potentials. Older workers can educate and model to younger workers their work ethic, and on the traditions of the company. Younger workers can serve to educate older employees on technologies of the modern age and how to best apply them.

Accommodating Different Work Patterns

More and more changes are being observed in today's workforce. The traditional 9-5 working period may not be as viable and productive in this age and time as it was in the late 20th Century. Millennials and Gen X workers are more interested in working different hours to enhance work productivity, as well as handle the stresses of life outside of the job.

How to Build a Positive Company Culture

If executives must invest in one thing, that should be company culture. It is an ingredient that propels employee engagement, resulting in both internal and external growth, as well as a high level of productivity. Culture is the shoulder on which rests the values of the company and how people perceive the company and what it does.

Most experts and proponents like Hung Pham, the Culture Summit founder and a host of other professionals give their insights on how to effectively develop a company culture. Whatever it is, every company has a company culture, whether it is consciously built, or not, because companies do not exist in a vacuum. No matter what the current culture of the company is, a better one can be built with these factors in mind:

1. The Brand Story: Make Employees a Part of It

Every company brand has a story behind it. Far beyond simply helping to attract customers to the business, the brand story is a viable tool to develop the culture. The brand shapes the employees' minds and aligns them to play their part in it. Brand stories can be very powerful, showing employees the reason they are doing what they are employed to do.

The employer has to clearly define the company story, but the employees are part of it and will appreciate getting to understand things better to better facilitate the achievement of the company's dreams. Whatever concept or culture that the company desires to go with, employees should fully understand how they fit into the brand story and play their parts with enthusiasm and ownership.

Dan Spaulding of the Zillow Group emphasizes that company executives should intentionally use explicitly clear language to enlighten employees about company values, missions, and workplace practices. Spaulding further describes the mission statement or list of values --- they shouldn't be just words on the walls of the building; rather they should precede all meetings and be a part of all critical decisions of the company. Hone it in messages and memos. From this emphasis, the new employees will be sure of what they're getting into and should gain the confidence to perform to corporate expectations and values. Other employees who have been around longer won't find it difficult aligning with a more defined company culture.

2. Be Consistent But Flexible

Change is bound to happen in life. The same applies to companies. There is the possibility of increasing change in technology and company growth. Culture should not be rigid. Though the company's core values should always be consistent, culture can be treated as a flexible tool but should always align with company goals.

3. Prioritize People

People who work in the company are an invaluable resource to treasure. The first and main focus should always be on your people. There should be company-wide engagement --- none should be neglected. At first, whether during the recruitment or training process, the employer needs to put the "round peg in round holes," ensuring that each new hire is the right fit for the job and the team, and should consider themselves as belonging to the company community. This drives success and helps people focus on what they were hired to do.

The employer can't afford to not treat the employees well if building a positive culture matters at all to the organization. Company culture can only be negative when employees are not well taken care of. All employees need to be in their best mental, physical, and emotional state to make a continuous good impact on the company and further develop its culture. Leaders should make sure to provide the enabling environment, tools, resources and other expressed needs identified by the employees themselves to function at the highest levels in the workplace. People ultimately determine the company's success, so prioritize them.

4. Encourage a Collaborative Spirit

A company desiring growth should be regarded as a family where everybody works together. The employer should motivate everyone involved to work as a team and not individually. A good business team --- just like a winning sports team --- places the company and the team at the top of considerations when a situation arises that calls for a choice or during a conflict. Even in the face of disagreement, it is done in good faith to favor the company. This assertion is supported by Amazon's Web Services Head of Product, Tatyana Mamut. She believes company leaders are held together by the power of common vision.

5. Provide Meaning

Both purpose and meaning are vital in the workplace; everyone in the organization should be able to articulate the reasons why they are in the company. No company builds a culture without employees having a solid grasp of these two vital considerations.

6. Let Everyone Take Part in Setting Goals

Clear goals impact strongly on how the employees can quickly align with the culture. Employers should work together with their teams to come up with the company's objectives and goals. Let everybody in the various teams have their unique duty to work towards. Not having clear goals for the company is comparable to not knowing the purpose of the company's existence, making it like piloting a rudderless ship.

7. Improve Social Connections

Social relations in the workplace are critical to building a good culture. The employer can't expect to have a strong culture in an organization when employees hardly have the time, opportunity or permission to interact. Leaders should provide interactive opportunities among colleagues at the workplace. The institution of activities like happy hour outings, team meals, team decorations for holidays, etc. helps get everybody talking with one another. It helps collaboration which is an integral part of a successful company.

8. Be a Good Listener

Employers can make things easier on themselves by listening, and encouraging employees to contribute ideas, thoughts, and feelings about an issue. In a survey by CultureIQ, 86% of workers at establishments with a strong company culture say they have listening leaders compared to the 70% of companies that have weak or unhealthy cultures. Let the employees' voice count and treat them as valuable --- they will reciprocate with building a strong culture by their output and positive attitudes.

9. Encourage Culture Champions

Culture champions uplift the values and missions of the company, they know it in and out. They are probably older employees who have seen it all and know exactly what the company wants. These "culture champions" are almost always happy and strongly inspired to promote and motivate others to follow in their paths. Pick out these employees and empower them as much as possible.

10. Pay Attention to Future Recruitment

Don't just hire. Employ only individuals that fit the company. Recruitment should not be based on technical abilities alone; culture consideration should be one of the top requirements. Hire top talents that are the best fit for the job mentally, professionally and socially and interact well with others inside and outside the company.

Changing Company Culture the Employer No Longer Wants

Change is a constant thing in life, often posing huge obstacles, even in the best of times. Changing a company culture is not easy either; it is one of the most difficult challenges leadership in an organization has to grapple with. This is because a culture is an interwoven set of processes, goals, rules, communication practices, values and principles that have been built over a long period since the organization was established.

But sometimes, changes are right and prudent. To change a culture is simply identifying the problem and taking action to effect the change. There should be no hard and fast rules about this process of culture change. This scenario below explains how a company can change the culture.

A senior leader once requested she wanted a change in the organizational culture. The professional service firm she runs is people-driven, but she realized her employees were not happy. [3] However, the firm is successful! It generates good revenue, has hard-working and efficient employees, and excellent client patronage. But the downside is that employee satisfaction was suffering and retaining good workers was difficult. According to her, employees were delivering but were not staying long. It turns out the firm in question had built up a reputation and culture of being an unfriendly place to work.

A leader under the senior leader expressed that their cultural practices were leading to profits, but that they were losing some of their most productive employees. He gave an instance of a case that involved an employee who had to attend a client meeting on her wedding day before she was allowed to attend her wedding. That is a textbook example of a toxic company culture! Such a culture is not sustainable, because eventually they will lose their most valuable assets --- their employees. A change in culture would be welcome here!

To make these changes, conscious moves are needed and must be carefully implemented. However, the changes should not be directed to the performance review system, the career training programs, the reward packages, or other benefits.

Two straightforward procedures can be adopted to implement these changes. They both revolve around stories. First, the employer actively gets involved in an event that is story-worthy, which fully represents the culture that is to be changed. After its implementation, allow other employees to tell a story around it.

Secondly, the employer finds among the employees those who have engaged in a story-worthy event that represents the culture to be implemented. Then the employer goes ahead and tells stories about them. Carefully taking action steps in the direction of the change should be the tactic of choice. Let employees see the difference in action in their workplaces and interactions, and not only posting a few nice-sounding words on the walls of the office.

Branding the Culture as Employer Branding

A company's brand speaks about its reputation. It says more about the services, products, and history and company executives, among other characteristics. It tends to be an inspiration for people who use the product, see and hear the ads, and become the mouthpiece to others, speaking either good or bad about the company. The brand is such a powerful tool that the employer should consistently have it in front of their mind.

The second kind of brand for consideration is employer branding. Employer branding is how prospective employees perceive the company. A positive employer branding is a must-have in this current age and time where the job market is so highly competitive. Retaining and recruiting the best people becomes challenging and rather expensive when positive branding is lacking. Creating the impression that a company is the best place to work in is what branding is all about. It covers everything from the salaries, benefits, working environment, treatment of employees, opportunities for advancement. Also, everything the employer wants to showcase to present an engaging work environment and to draw in great talent. If the employer is looking out for great resume's, you can also be assured that job seekers are equally looking out for a great employer. Branding helps immensely in this regard.

Letting the Company Culture Drive the Employer Branding

Telling a good story about the company and portraying the organization in a good light in the marketplace sells the company to the workforce the employer wants to become part of the company. The story the employer tells should be about the culture and its values. The employer must consciously infuse this in the employer branding.

It's not really the company presenting a good impression; it is more about the employer living out the story he communicates. Remember Glassdoor --- the employer's real reviews are available for public scrutiny. If the company wants to attract top-quality workers, then they must get it right with the branding. The good thing is that the brand can be continually tweaked, and that is where the company culture gets into the act.

Give Attention to the Career Website

Everything the employer has on their site should reflect the culture of the company. The content, the design --- really everything about the website should give the right reflection of what the organization is and what it would be like to work there. Make sure to highlight the Employee Value Proposition (EVP)--- the reward system, benefits, policies, and career development programs. They should be prominent on the site to attract prospects. Let prospects see the credibility of the company, showcase videos, testimonials, and existing employee stories. This document lets prospective employees understand what the company is like in real life. Let the job description be apparent to the readers.

Utilize the Power of Social Media

The company profile speaks volumes about the employer branding; so put forth a lot of effort to make it stand out. In today's world, the employer can't ignore the power of social media platforms. It is estimated that about 25% of most job seekers use social media as a primary tool in researching potential employers [4]. How the employer introduces the company culture into employer branding is up to the employer on the channels he chooses to be active on.

Employee Branding: Walk the Talk

Companies desire to have a strong brand and loyalty-base to retain their existing customers. Employees are the first contact with the customers in the workplace, and so branding becomes a critical issue for a company.

Many company executives are interested in how branding their employees can yield good dividends and provide an edge over their competitors. It's all wrapped up in the company's culture. As in employer branding, employee branding is about positively presenting a company before job seekers, employees, stakeholders, and potential customers.

In their research paper, W.Glynn and Sandra Miles came up with a definition that best fits into the employee branding process [5]. They view the act as the process by which employees adopt the company's brand image, projecting it to customers and other company stakeholders.

Employee branding goes a long way to showcase the company's unique assets. The effort put into employee branding is worth it when measured against the positives it brings to the company. It gives the public, prospective employees, and would-be customers a picture of what the company is via the crop of people who drive its operation.

Employee branding even comes into play through media exposure. Take a look at the correspondents of the Cable News Network (CNN) as an example, and the employer will see the impact of employee branding on their behaviors, and carriage. They leave the employer in no doubt that they are a substantial part of the company and are walking in line with the culture of the establishment. The employer can see them conclude their reports beaming with confidence as they sign off with, "This is CNN." Companies that get things right with a dependable employee branding status can make their employees stars and brand ambassadors of the company.

Employees must protect the organization's image before customers and stakeholders. They play a significant role in effectively positioning the organization regardless of whether a negative image exists alongside it or not. They are brand ambassadors and should be enlightened on the importance of their roles.

It is the role of the employer to shape all employees' behavior such that people who work for the organization can creatively project the company's image and its identity in a positive light via their social media publication and general behavior within the company and externally.

Employees can walk the talk about the company they work with by putting up a robust brand engagement on the social media network where the company profile is displayed. They should become active participants on those platforms, 'liking' the pages and leaving positive comments on Facebook, Instagram, Twitter, and others.

CHAPTER TWO

How to Find True Talents and Make Them Blossom

They are the gifted few in the educational sector; in the corporate world, employers pride them as true talents. Human Resources (HR) view them as an invaluable asset in their organization. Company executives will agree that true talents are scarce resources and that, when found, all effort must be taken to retain them. Company leaders know the place of true talents in their establishment; they tend to add something extra to the overall operation of the organization. They are worth every bit of their wages and the benefits package the company set aside to make them stay much longer in the company.

Indeed talented employees are great tools in the hands of company management to achieve their set goals. As rare employees, they are the pillars behind well-established companies. If there is anything company leaders ought to be doing with these valued individuals in their fold, it is how to make them shine. And if genuinely exceptional workers are missing in a company's employee ranks, then finding them should be a task of great importance. There is so much to say about the value of true talents.

All employees represent the company as brand ambassadors and play distinct roles. But the exceptional team members pull together and are such an attractive force that they tend to draw customers closer to the company. They make good things happen when it seems that a problem appears insurmountable. The productivity of these talented people is rated far higher than other regular staff in a company.

A research publication shows that including a single star performer in a team boosts the effectiveness of the group by between 5% and 15%.[6] No wonder why many top organizations invest massively in finding the top talents around the world to fill the most sensitive positions. Whether the company is in the business of making profits or is a non-profit or Non-Governmental Organization (NGO) performing essential tasks to make the world better, talents still make these various organizations reach far beyond where they ultimately want to be in the shortest possible time.

Some employees are born talents; others are self-made. They may be few but still account for a large output in the organization. Their performance tends to increase as the task difficulty increases. They exhibit high-performance attitudes and energy so much that they affect the production of others in the team. Company leaders will do well if this crop of employees gets placed in the right positions in the organization.

There shouldn't be any doubt that outstanding achievers will perform and drive others to achieve the set goals of the company. They are comparable to the influencers in the digital marketing world when one or two are found in a team. They are team builders that breed confidence in others wherever they are in the company. Employers, HR managers, and supervisors do everything to find and retain this set of individuals in their company. But how do they locate these high performers and get them to come on board when they are so hard to find?

The Talent Hunt

Among several challenges confronting leadership in a company, attracting and retaining the best talent stands as one. Corporate leaders agree that not all employees are the same; some are naturally more gifted and talented than the others. But aside from the professional skills and work ethic, the new hire must also fit the company culture. Mark the phrase, 'company culture.' The real talents you seek should be those who will fit in your company culture. That is the best way to make them blossom and grow in your operational model.

Remember the days when phrases such as "talent wars" and others were popular; it all boils down to how difficult it was --- and still is --- to find great talents that will fit into a company's culture. Leadership experts advise employers not to settle for less, but to seek out only the very best if they wish to build a company that stands out in the crowd. Apple's Steve Jobs recommended employers to go hard after the cream of the cream, the best prospects available in the market.[7]

How to Do the Search

There are various ways to find individuals to fill multiple positions in an organization. The mistake many employers make is to take their search outside the company to the labor market, ignoring what they have within. Internalizing talent search should be considered first.

When on the hunt, employers should not rely on experience as a significant parameter. Though it should not be discounted, it also shouldn't be a core requirement. The best employees or talents are naturally motivated and enthusiastic individuals far beyond what only experience indicates. The employer should look beyond the high-positioned employees within their employee ranks. Employers should demonstrate a flexible approach in their deliberations, and give every employee the benefit of the doubt when searching for that personality that displays the talent they seek.

Hidden talents abound in all companies; they only need the enabling environment and encouragement to shine. It should be noted that such employees may require motivation and be consciously guided to come out of their shell. Leaders should see this as a primary ongoing duty to dig out the hidden jewels in their company and position them in their rightful place in the organization.

In contrast, employers can get the best out of the hiring process by recruiting employees that show potential, and then polishing them to perform optimally. Yes, there are latent talents who themselves don't know what abilities they have. These employees can even be recruited as entry-level staff. Executives with the 'eagle eye' will spot the latent talents in these recruits and bring them in to fill a position where they will perform at their best. This might even entail that some rules, such as in length of time on the job, seniority protocols, etc. will need to be broken. There are hidden talents in every company just waiting to be discovered and turned into a star for a company's benefit. Just how these talents are found can be done in a variety of ways.

Steps to Fish out True Talents From the Crowd

Give a Test

Talents distinguish themselves with their exceptional organizational, professional, and interpersonal abilities. These abilities are the primary criteria to identify potential shakers and movers in the workforce. By testing, it is not necessarily going to be a formal kind of examination. It should be administered during regular working hours. Leaders should keenly watch how employees carry out their duties. They shouldn't even be aware that they are being tested; that is the intent. The point here is the skills and knowledge demonstrated by the employee in executing a job in everyday average work-life. Employers can have this assessment on their employees via a task sample.

Also, leaders should take into account the reasoning potentials of such individuals. That is, how feasible it would be for the employee to execute more complex tasks in the future. For instance, the potential in an employee to fit into a leadership role can be determined based on the employee's strategic thinking and their potential to adapt to the company's plans. Entrepreneurial strength and collaborative attitude also set true talents apart. Team spirit is an integral part of any organization; don't ignore this in a talent search. Of course, this soft skill can be improved in an employee who has demonstrated robust qualities that fit in the role being scouted for.

Look Beyond Career Levels

It is pretty convenient to pick up several employee files and to categorize them purely on experience and length of service. That isn't the right way to go if you're going to pick out hidden talents in the company. The forward-thinking entrepreneur will need to work hard to break old mindsets, so they are more objective in finding those hidden gems that may be right under their noses. This is preferred rather than just promoting those with the best sales records or some such metric.

Employers will see the truth in the argument that some top-ranked employees still fail in their management skills and have lower performance rates. Some research findings show that for every two leaders, at least one is unable to engage with employees effectively.[8] This goes to show that selecting true talents based only on job titles may not be the best parameter to use.

The experience level and academic knowledge of a particular employee should not be placed as the most critical factor here; employers should search for employees with outstanding potential future performance. Hunting for talents should be based on capabilities and personal attributes instead, including things like Emotional Quotient (EQ).

Work Ethics

Most talents in the workplace separate themselves from their peers with their work ethics. They are hard-working, motivated, and have this 'never say die' spirit; they won't give up on a difficult task until they find a solution. They bring in this strong drive that affects others positively to run along with the task at hand. Values such as strong motivation, hard work, and the will to get the job done in the face of difficulty are features to look for. Top performers are often dissatisfied with lackluster performance; they are driven to attain great achievement in their roles. When recommendation and recognition for performance are awarded, they are always in the lead of others on their level.

Behavioral characteristics are a significant factor here also. Employers should note how hard an employee is willing to work and their readiness to take up more jobs as needed. Is such an employee showing a considerable amount of responsibility and the availability for tasks at odd periods? Is the employee willing to sacrifice for the company's good? Many issues regarding work ethics should be considered when searching out for the right people for promotion.

Management Skills

Management skills are entangled in an employee's social abilities. Working in an organizational environment is about a relationship with others, and management skills are about relating to humans --- decreasing conflicts while enhancing camaraderie and cooperation.

Employers can look at this criterion from the angle of the ability to manage others and as well as their self-management. Good relationships and the ability to interact with others is a strong force in a company's growth. Employees who have the potential to succeed in more prominent roles can confidently manage themselves to withstand undue pressure. They also have a solution to complex tasks and show a high level of confidence in the positions they occupy. All of these are embodied in a strong emotional intelligence ability (EQ) of the employee.

Company executives, supervisors, and the management team can make true talents out of their employee teams as a starting point to finding the most skilled individuals to fill a position. The advantage of this approach is that such employees already know the culture of the company --- they only need refinement and given better orientation in the new role they will be playing.

Now that the employer has identified their best and brightest, what ways should be used to bring out the best in them?

How to Make Talents Shine

The task of discovering talents begins from a well-coordinated search, but it doesn't stop there. The real work comes in their development and training so they can perform at their best. As important as the identification of top performers may be, the discovery only helps to bring in a set of individuals who need refining to perform to the best of their abilities. Company leaders must help such talents shine and fully utilize all of their personality and professional traits to the company's benefit.

Employers have probably hired employees because there are some hidden talents seen in them. Leaders must instill company values and mission into their prospective skills; building them up to carry the organization on their shoulders as ambassadors of the brand. It's not rocket science; every company leader can quickly get this done. There are essential steps employers can go about to achieve this. Let's examine those now.

Use Affirmation to Provide Motivation

Working under pressure is a part of the modern workplace, but it doesn't have to be in most cases. The majority of employees don't give their best performance in high-pressure situations. Leaders should not use forceful or harsh words on employees; it will kill their spirit. To pat an employee on the back does not pamper workers but instead helps to encourage them to keep learning from mistakes and take some risks for potential benefits to the company. Thus, workers are more encouraged to 'think outside the box' when confronted with problems.

Training

Training is a process to improve employee performance. Generally, training should be a continuous process regardless of whether it is directed at helping maximize the talents of top performers or not. Necessarily, this should be a significant part of every company culture. Employers should not fall for the trap that many hold onto about the training process: Some believe high-potential workers are bound to leave the organization any time they choose to so that the time and effort placed on training would be wasted. That should not deter employers from doing the right thing when the need calls for it.

Henry Ford made a profound statement on this: "The only thing worse than training your employees and having them leave is not training them and having them stay."[9] If employers find value in their discovered talents, having a budget for this purpose shouldn't be viewed as a burden. Company leaders should train and retrain. The in-house training should be tailored after talent discovery needs.

In the talent training process, the focus should not just be learning new skills. Trainees may be required to unlearn a particular method and relearn an already existing principle to have a better understanding of how it applies in their specific role in this company. The learning process should be a comprehensive one that brings together the three arms of learning: learn, unlearn, and relearn to become the perfect fit for the desired role.

Show Faith

There is no better way to deal with a discovered talent than to show trust in the abilities of the employee. Employers have to carry this with them daily. Leaders should have in mind that these attributes will influence their dealings with all their employees. When positive thoughts dominate through contact, language, and actions, it should encourage such employees to be at their best. If leaders don't believe in what a potential talent can add to the company, such an employee will likely not give their best at the workplace. Leaders should consciously communicate to these high performers the faith and confidence they have in them so the employee can utilize their potential to the fullest.

Clarify Goals

Highly-motivated employees want to run with a given goal when they fully understand it. Understanding the task before them aids the employee to feel a part of the whole process. They will, therefore, take greater ownership of each job assignment to make sure to meet the target for each task or project.

Employers won't get the best from their newly discovered talents when a job description or the company's goals for a project are confusing. If an employer comes with a contradicting statement or gives directives that are difficult to follow, job performance from the employees will be at risk. Complexity should be replaced with simplicity.

Reward Performance

Working can be a pain, and not everybody delights in doing it very hard. But that can change when a morale booster in the form of a reward is attached to every completed task/project. There is this instinct in every human to want to do more and achieve at high levels when they know a reward is sitting around the corner for outstanding performance.

Do employers desire to see their employees produce outstanding goods and services? Then they should have a codified reward system in place to encourage optimum performance.

Getting the best out of people can come when the organization rewards efforts and performance. Rewards and awards can be distributed to the best performing staff monthly, quarterly, or annually. And the rewards do not have to be monetary. Recognition and special commendations in a general meeting can serve as the tonic the employee needs for better performance. Many individuals will probably value this kind of recognition above monetary incentives.

Deal with Employees Honestly

Humans feel safe when they are with people who are known to be honest. Employers should be more open with their employees, expressing to them that everyone has weaknesses and strengths. Let employees know that a deficiency in an area is not necessarily a total negative; because understanding a particular flaw helps that individual to complement their teammates in other areas where they do excel.

Workers are more willing to rise to the tasks when leaders deal with them with an open mind. Trust and honesty are two closely-related virtues leaders can't leave to chance when dealing with people. Trust and honesty work both ways in the employer-employee relationship, and benefits both.

Assign Greater Responsibilities

Assigning greater responsibilities to the potential talents stretches their ability, strengthens their skills and helps them add new ones. Leaders can do this in several ways. Let the employee direct the next meeting or give a presentation on a given project. Greater responsibilities mean extra commitment, and this is where talents explode to bring out their hidden potential.

Show Care

This is absolutely an invaluable need. Employees are not all the same. To develop talents, employers should treat every employee differently. Care to know what they may be going through in their lives if that will help. It is not out of place that the employee has some issues in their lives that affect their work. Leaders should not lose the connection, some days off can be given to such employees to let them recover and get back on track. This works pretty well to help talents always on their toes to perform.

Prioritize the Culture of Reaching Greater Heights

Leaders should drive the success spirit into the talent. Make the talent to not see any good in mediocrity. Enable talents through available tools and allow a free hand to fully express their abilities. Allow talents to push their limits. Put them through a tough challenge, and this will sharpen their skills and make them do better.

Allow Employees to Express Themselves

When leaders give room to their staff to express themselves, they perform better --- flexibility is the name of the game these days. Great talents always have a better way to approach a given task, so allow some measure of freedom. Doing this empowers them to see value in their abilities and how significant their contribution is to the company. They will naturally rise to the occasion when called upon to solve a problem.

Employers and Talent Management

Organizations have talents within the company, and the labor market boasts of an array of skills in diverse industries. There is one more thing to add after hiring the needed staff members to an organization, and this is the focus on how your staff are managed.

Talent management in an organization is the approach an employer takes to retain and make the best use of the talented and skilled workforce in the company. It also entails the steps and commitment to develop and optimize the workforce in the establishment. Proper management begins from the very moment the organization thinks about recruiting new talents and goes on to the everyday activities in the workplace.

Talent management comprises recruitment, job description development, application materials review, on-the-job training, credential review, employee onboarding, job termination process, and employee development --- among others.

Talent management covers HR processes, including advertising for open positions, evaluating and hiring, and then holding on to well-performing employees in the organization. This implies that talent management begins with the hiring process down to when the recruit is integrated into the company, and on through to retirement or termination.

Human Resources and company leaders have a duty to manage the talents in the company properly. A workable strategy must be in place for this. These practices include:

- How employees' progress is measured and improved
- Management of performance
- Retention of high-performing employees
- Training and professional development
- Reward system and incentives for excellent performance
- The onboarding process
- Healthy employee engagement at the workplace
- Succession plan

As should be evident from the above, it takes a conscious effort from an employer to have in place adequate talent management. The goal is to make the employee a better worker and as well as reduce staff turnover.

Global Talent Hunt

All that has been discussed so far has focused on finding talents within the company. However, employers may have to go outside their fold to find the needed abilities to fill a position. It doesn't come easy most times for many employers. Locating and hiring the most valuable employee possible can be sometimes expensive, risky, time-consuming, and may not be a cultural fit for the individuals to be employed. Most employers would rather pass this responsibility on to a third-party hiring agency so that they can concentrate on other pressing needs in the company.

The obvious truth is that genuinely exceptional employees are rare entities in the labor market world. It may be through the usual job postings, but employers should adopt creativity in the talent search if they truly want to find the right fit for the position they have vacant.

Network with Others

Leaders can take advantage of people they already know to help refer to a potential new hire. This method works pretty well in most cases. Friends in the specific industrial sector they belong can suggest talents they can personally vouch for. Referral methods have long existed; and it should not be surprising to know that a majority of companies adopt this approach to get some of the high-performing talents to join their organizations.

LinkedIn Works

Social media is actively involved in every area of our lives. Particularly, LinkedIn stands out as a professional tool that many hiring managers rely on. One can call LinkedIn to the job board for the internet age, and you won't be far wrong. Less professionally inclined platforms such as Facebook and Twitter also have their fair share of success in assisting employers in finding their prospective talents.

Meet-Ups and Conferences

Meeting the right talent can be when leaders find themselves in the right places at the right times. Conferences, seminars, and other similar events offer leaders a golden opportunity to meet large pools of possible prospects that probably share the same skills and experiences as in one's own company. These conferences can provide a pleasant atmosphere where industry-related groups converge and connect.

Utilize Contests

A contest is one viable way to search out talents for a company in the larger labor market. The entertainment sector does this very well; at least this is visible in the music industry. Popular programs like 'America's Got Talent' and 'UK's Got Talent' are well-known contests that have made many stars in the music industry.

The contest for finding the most talented employees may not necessarily be run like the ones above. For instance, employers can find great talents by using contests on various freelance platforms. Present a problem to be solved on the board and allow contributions from freelancers who are experienced in the sector and have the minimum prerequisite qualifications that are desired. Pick out as many solutions as meets the need. Monetary incentives will surely come into play here, but employers should look far beyond that. They should find a way to reach them and be mindful of the platform's rules on appropriate contact modes.

Have in mind that some of these freelancers are experienced and professionals in their fields who are looking to find an excellent opportunity to exercise their talents --- but simply haven't found one yet. Employers should make sure they alert professionals in their region about the contest as a requirement since those people work physically with the company.

Use Recruiters

Professional recruiters still work very well. The reason for this is, they have a huge pool of job seekers to work from. Employers may not have all the time to go through such a process, but finding reputable professional recruiters will surely help. Companies only need to consider the best employees with the qualities they most value, and leave the rest to the recruiters to work through. Of course, this service will come with an extra expense for the company.

Leverage Existing Employees Network

Existing staff within the company will have friends who could prove to be the very addition needed by the organization. Leaders should ask their staff members for their referrals. It may be surprising when they provide one or two individuals who excel in the abilities you want to be filled.

After all is said and done, and your new talents are discovered, employers' next move should be a good onboarding process.

CHAPTER THREE

Why an Onboarding Process Is Needed

So, the employer finally found a true talent after a thorough search. No doubt, a lot of energy, time, and resources have been exerted and have finally paid off. When the hunt for finding talents has ended, then the onboarding starts.

Welcoming the new employees and helping them succeed should be on the lips of leaders at this stage. Onboarding takes care of this. It is a crucial process for every establishment.

However, a big challenge that employers are confronted with is how easily new employees leave the company within a very short time after being hired. The reason for this can be attributed to the unpleasant working experience in their very first weeks or months in the new company.

In the US, for example, about 33% of new employees start searching for new jobs within just six months of their current employment. The percentage is even higher among millennials. Before their first anniversary, 23% of new employees say they would have left the company if they could.[10] What could be the cause? A critical look into how the new hires were introduced into the company needs to be investigated. Are managers not having sufficient time to deal with the situation? Many things can be responsible, but it all boils down to the onboarding adopted by the organization for new employees. The truth is, it takes a whole lot of commitment and effort to help the new hires become fully integrated into the company. The onboarding process is crucial because not doing it effectively is as bad as not having a process in place at all.

The Onboarding Process

The onboarding process is the activities that help to integrate the newly employed to the company. It continues for an extended period to support the new employee to become fully established in the company. The employee is given the necessary information, appropriate tools to use, and how to get things done in their new position in the organization. The goal is to make the employee feel at home in the workplace and to be productive.

Ineffective onboarding is a serious issue that the employer must take time to deal with for the hiring process to be most fruitful. It should be mentioned that it is the most crucial program in the life of a new hire. Why? The reason is that it has a significant impact on their future performance, engagement with the company, and increases the length of tenure with the organization.

A large percentage of employees are less likely to leave a company when they are fully engaged in the company. The starting point to this feat is adequately acquainting the new employee with the work environment from the very earliest stages of their employment --- before their actual start date. If new arrivals are well-integrated into a company, by understanding its culture and values and able to play their role in the position they are employed, then the desire on the employee's part to leave due to dissatisfaction with the job will be significantly reduced.

Onboarding should not be confused with the orientation program, both complement each other. The orientation program is a part of the onboarding process. It is not proper to forego an onboarding program all because a company has an orientation program in place. It really should be the other way round. While an orientation program usually introduces the employee to the organization in one day, onboarding takes months and even years --- depending on the position and complexity of the job description. Every employer needs a robust onboarding program if a new hire's success, retention, and productivity are desired.

A recent Harvard Business Review article [11] states that a well-structured onboarding will contain:

- A one-on-one type of jumpstart coaching with exhaustive support and feedback
- Introduce new employees to other workers, so they are comfortable and feel at home in the workplace
- Have an adequate and consistent follow-up
- Need for a thorough introduction to the use of the company's technology

Via onboarding, companies equip new employees with the knowledge and orientation they need to understand the working environment and soon start to contribute. Emphasis is placed on 'equipping'; this is what allows the new employees to function in the roles in which they are appointed.

The Right Time for Onboarding

By onboarding effectively, company leaders should know they are taking care of their future employees as they should so they quickly become a part of the team. This is one of the reasons why onboarding shouldn't start when an employee is hired; it should begin right before hiring someone. It goes on from there to when the person is assigned to their team and they take up their first assignment in the office. It doesn't stop at that point though but continues for such time until the employee is wholly acclimated to both their job position and to the company as a whole.

Some may argue about the right time to start the onboarding process. My recommendation is that the process should start when the authority to hire for an open position has been received. Just as a family will prepare beforehand when they decide to have a baby, the onboarding also takes the same route.

Starting onboarding before the employee is hired allows the employer to put things in place physically for the new position or the vacant position to be replaced. Preparing items ahead before hiring means the company is set to employ. This is part of the onboarding.

Questions such as: Is there an office space to accommodate the new employee? Is there any desk assigned if it is an open office? Is there other office equipment such as telephone, computer, and other tools available in their rightful place that needs attending to before ever considering hiring? Contact should be made to the necessary personnel, such as the IT departments to set up connections properly. Things must be set out clearly for the office to be created or position to be occupied. Even if the new employee has to sign for the materials to be used in his office, provision has to be made for this beforehand --- not when the new hire arrives for their first day.

Company leaders who hope to beat the competition should be mindful here; because their employer branding status will be on trial, so to speak. The smooth transition through proper onboarding will speak volumes to the new employee on arrival. If any one thing is more helpful in this first stage, it is having a checklist in place to put things right.

Importance of Onboarding

For the sake of both the new hires and the company; the new employee is settled in at the workplace in an efficient time and armed with the tools and knowledge to succeed in their new positions will relieve stress on established employees and the new hires, plus the company benefits from the productivity at once.

The skill gaps between old employees and new recruits cause the new employee to lack confidence, which often leads to the employee leaving the company abruptly. In contrast, in a report published by the Aberdeen Group, 77% of employees who participate in an onboarding process can attain their first job milestone in very little time when their performance is assessed.[12]

Some staggering facts on the need for employee onboarding are apparent reasons not to ignore the practice. In some of the research findings, it is recorded that onboarding can raise employee performance by as much as 11% and the retention of employees by 25%. Also, employees who are part of a well-structured onboarding are 69% more likely to stay with the organization for at least three years. It takes as much as 8-12 months for new employees to be at par in efficiency as established employees in the same role in the company without going through this process.[13] Furthermore, 15% of employees said ineffective onboarding is responsible for their quitting a job.

Onboarding is needed to establish a good measure of trust and relationship-building between managers and recruits. This enables both parties to freely discuss issues such as skill gaps and tools needed to succeed in the position they are appointed. This is possible through the one-on-one forum created in the onboarding program.

However, owing to the poor onboarding in many organizations, in a short time, employees who are struggling to find their feet at the workplace after two to three weeks --- or even a few months ---

will sooner or later want to try elsewhere. Considering the cost of the hiring process that companies incur, leaving out a proper onboarding should not be ignored by employers.

From another recent study, structured onboarding was shown to be not all about preparing new employees for their positions; it also encompasses employee engagement and building of their confidence at the most critical and sensitive point in their new careers. In a nutshell, onboarding is vital for the following reasons:

- It helps to retain employees much longer in the company
- It fosters employee productivity
- It is an educative process where employees are educated about their duties
- It cuts down on employee anxiety at the workplace

Making a Success of the Onboarding

Having seen how valuable onboarding can be, the employer should be more concerned about making a success out of it. The new employee should be settled and well-integrated into the company, knowing the roles to play and having the right tools to work with. After the employee has accepted the offer and before the start of work, here are additional things that can be done for successful onboarding.

Carry out Proper Documentation

Documentation of personal details is essential at this stage. Personal information such as name, contact address, social security number, and other relevant information needs to be documented. The employer should continuously stay in touch with the employee through emails or calls for the necessary documentation. This is even more like the familiarization process; new hires are comfortable with this.

Inform Other Departments

This time, notification is made to the other departments that will require some information or be aware of a new employee. The Payroll, HR, IT departments, and others who need information about the latest addition to the company should be contacted. Information about the new employee's name, start date, the title, should all be forwarded. Company leaders will do well to ensure preparation is made well ahead in these departments due to possible waiting lists before the employee arrives.

The IT department is probably most important at first. They must be instructed to create email accounts for the new employees and make sure to add them to the email list of the company, so they receive information during distribution. They shouldn't be left out when emails are sent.

Onboarding is very crucial; its importance can't be overemphasized. It can make orientation smooth and less stressful, or cause new employees to look for ways to leave the company. When the new employee finally starts work, the onboarding process doesn't stop. It goes on from the introduction and welcoming the employee to teammates and supervisors, down to the orientation and filling out of the necessary papers --- preferably everything in digital form --- and getting the worker set for the first assignment in the workplace.

Once again, a digital checklist will do the trick, so nothing is left out. Company leaders should know that this will rob from their employer branding status if things are not correctly handled. The employer doesn't have to wait for an employee to start work before beginning the onboarding. The sooner it begins, the better the possibility of integrating the employee as quickly as possible.

The Duration of the Onboarding Process

The question of how long the onboarding should last often comes up. This shouldn't be anything to worry about. The process may depend on the skill of the new arrival and the position to be occupied. A well-structured process should support the employee well enough to allow at least the new hire to pass the probationary review period. Conventionally, six or more months should be sufficient. It is always tricky when talents leave the company.

Considering the amount of time and resources expended on them, everything should be done to retain their services in the company. There should not be a limited period for onboarding --- changes in life today are also a part of the workplace. The performance management and HR units should determine to some extent how far the onboarding can continue. Will it ever end? Formally, it can, but the fact remains that learning is a continuous process, and the employee can continue to learn all through their service time with the organization.

How to Carry out a Well-Structured Onboarding

Having new employees to be fully integrated with the company takes a while; patience is the principle to watch out for. The first few days are highly influential in the life of the new employee. Employers are looking at ways to enhance employee performance, retain them, and help provide the satisfaction all workers desire in the workplace.

We all now know that onboarding should begin very early. Below are other guidelines that should be followed.

1. Set Goals and Expectations in Good Time

Not being sure about what is expected from them is a new hire's nightmare. New employees want to be aware of their expected performance and goals. A recent LinkedIn survey made it clear that knowledge about performance goals comes second as the most critical aspect of onboarding. Goal setting and keeping new hires abreast of the goals and timelines allow new hires to evaluate themselves. This is where building a relationship with new employees comes into play, particularly between direct managers and employees. Employers should take the time to also listen to new employees. They should hear them out on these new goals, whether they fully understand what is expected of them. Communication is the fundamental principle here.

2. Spending Time with Direct Managers

One-on-one time with direct managers ranks high as a valuable aspect of the onboarding experience according to polls from LinkedIn. The technique is very effective, as 96% of respondents affirmed that the one-on-one session is the most rewarding experience they had during their acclimation process.[14] The forum offers a good ground for new employees to build a stable working relationship with the management. This is the kind of strong support many new hires look for in the company they are about joining.

3. Pair New Hires with Established Employees to Learn the Ropes

Yet another move toward making new employees comfortable is helping them learn "insider tips." For a new employee, nothing beats finding a dependable seasoned employee to rest on for guidance. Company leaders should pair new employees with established employees. This helps them to gel with the team and encourage the collaborative spirit. New hires should be exposed to other teams to aid faster development and skills required to perform along with others.

4. Placing High Esteem on Company Culture and Values

Getting new employees to fit into the company culture is very critical to onboarding. New employees will often fail to deliver on their duties for lack of fitting in with their teammates and immediate supervisors. In fact, it is reported that a high percentage of recruits fail to reach expected job standards as a result of this. The employer should, therefore, prioritize the company culture in the onboarding. The sharing of the relevant content of the company culture in the social media channels of the company is key to this.

New hires should be included in events; their welcome package should contain the history and culture that the company portrays. Employers must make sure that the company's mission statements, principles, and employee conduct guide are all set out for the new employee.

To make sure that only individuals with a seamless fit for the company culture continue, some organizations may pay-off newly hired employees who, during the onboarding, are discovered they don't fit in. The practice of fully integrating a new employee is a process. The steps must be carefully taken to achieve success, ensuring the new hire fits into the company goals. But the need for a complete onboarding process is instrumental for every growing organization.

Digital Onboarding

As the heading here implies, digital onboarding is a process that is at least partially available online. As we move towards a more digital world, we should expect to see more of the onboarding process go digital also. Employees should not sit in an empty office or elsewhere, filling in paper forms. No, this must be made professional in a digital way because that is what employees expect these days --- at least if we ask the youngest workers in the corporate world.

Here are a few quick points to consider in the digital onboarding:

1. It is easier to track what employees have completed and what remains.
2. If anything is missing, it will be easy to identify.
3. It is cost-effective. There is no need to print paper or other materials.
4. The onboarding can take place even before the new employee has started if there is an agreement made with the employer. The importance of an early onboarding has been stated above.
5. All employees will get the same documents, policies, and other files. No alternative versions will be necessary.

CHAPTER FOUR

Hiring Gig Workers - The Pros and Cons

No doubt, the labor market as it stands today, has a variety of laborers in the workforce. The operational mode of employees is more dynamic. Terms such as 'ad hoc staff' and temporary employees are not new in the corporate organization; managers explore these options anytime they need some helping hands outside their regular workforce. And with the advancement in technology and the power of the internet that allows companies to reach a global audience, this type of workforce is now more accessible than ever before. They are designed in different shapes and give room to a wide range of workers --- skilled and semi-skilled --- people who choose to work part-time and those who take the trade full-time. The work-at-home parent gives credence to this. If the word nursing mother has taken root, we may as well expect nursing fathers to join in the category. One will argue that working in the comfort of one's home is fast gaining ground, and is more profitable for those who have the skills that sell. The gig economy is a new and growing economy that has its advantages as well as disadvantages. Should this avenue be the channel that corporate leaders have been waiting for to help their businesses grow? What exactly is the 'gig economy,' the workers, its scope, benefits, and disadvantages?

Gig Workers and the Gig Economy

There are no gig workers without the gig economy that runs the show. The gig economy is a vibrant one growing from phase to phase. When employers understand how the gig economy operates, they will know how to appropriate its benefits for their company's development.

The term 'gig' was born from the world of performing arts. Musicians and comedians use it frequently to describe their services in the sector. When such professionals are called up to appear in a show or event which is paid for, the term 'gig' is usually used to describe the task. It may originate from the offline scene but now applies more over the internet.

The gig economy is a market system where individuals with various skills contract out their services to traditional or online businesses. It is a free market where people work and get paid without necessarily being the staff of a company. They are freelancers who undertake both core and minor tasks depending on the company hiring their services. Usually, the number of gigs a gig worker can sell determines the total income made.

Freelancing has long existed in traditional businesses. However, today's gig economy sector has some uniqueness to it as it incorporates more digitization. To the gig workers, the practice gives them the benefits of flexibility, a good measure of freedom, but does not come with any form of health or social benefits like for in-house staff. It depends on the specific gig agreement, of course. Freelancers must contend with the unique stresses that come with this type of employment. The good thing, though, is that the workers can choose to work part-time to complement their regular jobs; and growing numbers work as freelancers full-time. Regions with regular employment challenges turn to this thriving economy to earn a living.

Working independently doesn't come that easy for gig workers, because they have to take full responsibility for what is essentially their own self-owned business. It can be hard for beginners as it takes so much effort to convince clients to hire their services. If benefits are lacking and income is not guaranteed as in traditional employment, one can agree that working in the sector can be a struggle. It is not a picnic for many who have ventured into it. But despite some of the difficulties gig workers have to face, company leaders are opting more for gig workers for various reasons.

Signals That Send Companies to the Gig Economy

It appears to be the trend these days to find companies hiring more independent contractors to support their existing employees. In my experience in the corporate world, I have come to accept that the shortage of proficiency in a department could be a signal for employers to look outside the company to close up the gap. The gig economy is a large pool of experts in a different field. Many organizations believe that it is the quickest way to solve a problem that needs urgent attention; I can't help but agree with this assertion. Probably, the lack of sufficient funds to expand or hire talents can be the obstacle and why executives look in the direction of gig workers.

The need to beat the competition is yet another reason to reach out to gig workers. Many companies desire to scale up their businesses quickly. Outsourcing is undoubtedly a wise move to do this. Employers will approve that outsourcing less critical tasks to freelancers free up time and energy for the in-house staff to focus on more important things in the day-to-day running of the organization.

Sometimes, the reason for choosing to go to gig workers can be the difficulty in finding the right fit for a position in the company. When leaders notice that employees are losing their commitment to the company, it can be one of the signals for employers to act proactively. Executives may decide for this freelancer option as a precautionary move if an employee eventually leaves. A company that experiences very high amounts of turnover for whatever reason should see the good in having gig workers readily available. Is it true that these factors point to the sector as a goldmine where people can find jobs to meet their daily needs, or what exactly could be the positives to account for the growth factor we see today in the gig economy? Is the freelancing community growing at all?

The Gig Economy: How It Is Growing

Regardless of how challenging it may be starting in the gig economy for gig workers, this economy is on a growing trend. The data clearly shows promising growth in the years ahead.

It is reported that in 2018, 57 million Americans, that is, 36% of America's total workforce either engage part-time or full-time as gig workers, according to a recent Gallup study.[15] Does this not speak volumes of the growth level in the sector? If a whopping 57 million Americans alone are involved in the freelancing industry, there is so much to expect from the global participation in the economy.

Similarly, in the same Gallup report, the United States Bureau of Economic Analysis (BEA) gave an estimate that puts the growth of the digital economy to an average of 5.6 percent between 2006 and 2016. Keep in mind that the current gig economy is driven more by the digital system than it was back in 2006.

The number of individuals getting their income from the gig economy is continually increasing. Terms like 'side hustle' and the like give credence to this, pointing clearly to the fact that many people around the globe are now participating in the economy. Significantly, the freelancing sector is enjoying explosive growth, and in recent times more and more people are taking to 'gig-working.'

But why is this happening?

1. The Growth of Mobile Devices

Gig workers use their smartphones, computers, and other handheld devices for carrying out their duties. The digital world is going through a tremendous change, and so are digital devices. Before today, desktops and later laptops were computing devices used by comparatively few individuals who could afford them. Things have certainly changed!

According to the Pew Research Center, the growth of the gig economy will be much faster with the increasing use of mobile devices by people. Mobile apps are more popular, offering great possibilities to individuals. It is estimated by Digital Trends --- the online magazine --- that not less than 6.1 billion of the world's population will have at least one smartphone by 2020.[16] It goes to show that there is still more to come in this sector in terms of growth.

2. Globalization- a Major Contributor

People can sit in the comfort of their homes in far-away China and work for a client in America. Gig workers savor this privilege, and this is the main reason why the growth in the gig economy is steadily advancing. Unlike in the earlier years of the internet, most people are now familiar with basic computing skills and can take full advantage of what the online world has to offer.

3. Increased Patronage by Businesses

The gig economy is currently thriving as it stands because many companies --- small and large --- are seeing value in the use of gig workers. So, whatever the reasons may be that more company executives are turning to this new style of employee; skilled gig workers add value to the companies who use their services in terms of growth and cost savings.

4. The Changing Work Pattern

The business world is going through a transformation in terms of work-life. With the growing number of millennials beginning to dominate today's workforce, people willing to work long-term in an establishment is decreasing. And as work tilt towards working remotely, more and more people will be getting involved in the freelancing system by the day. Also, many of the most talented workers are more comfortable working for themselves as consultants, contract workers, and freelancers than to continue in regular employment.

5. Improvement in Technology

More than ever before, remote work and collaborative tools are readily available to facilitate an excellent working experience with contract staff. Many web-based platforms are springing up to offer these opportunities. Similarly, cloud-based technology has now made it possible for geographical locations to no longer be a factor in the availability of work to be found or work to be done. And the payment system is equally improved, with various online money processors helping.

6. Skills and Qualification

Skills are prioritized in the gig economy. This gives room to virtually anybody who has basic computer knowledge and has a marketable skill to get involved in the gig economy. This fact may be one of the vulnerabilities of the system, though; still, one cannot argue against its contribution to the growth of the economy. Advancement in technology and today's common work patterns, especially among the younger generation, is a strong force to the growth of the gig economy for the foreseeable future.

Long-term Employment: Younger Generation Thinks Differently

We've examined how work-life patterns among younger generations drive the growth of the gig workers. Why is that happening, and how do they see the long-term work-life? It is vital to beam the searchlight on the thoughts running through the minds of this crop of individuals on this age-long work-life approach.

In the past, it was fashionable to find employees work through their lifetime in a single organization. It would be hard to find many of today's younger generation who would want to work for the same company for 20 or more years. The working attitude is to change jobs at fairly frequent intervals. To talk about issues of pension and gratuity is alien to workers in their 20's and 30's; they are not at all interested in a lifestyle that ties them down to a particular environment and doing the same things over and over again for years. Dynamism and innovation are propelling factors that keep younger workers on their toes and on the move.

The gig working option is more attractive to millennials as it allows freedom to engage in other aspects of life that they view as equally important. Taking vacations, making new friends, traveling at will, and enjoying a work-life with people of similar passion are strong enticements for the younger generation to care less for long-term employment.

To buttress this point, a report found that 43% of people who were interviewed give the reason of having a flexible work schedule as the main factor in their decision to work as independent contractors.[17] Working on the go and anytime is like a dream come true --- the kind of lifestyle they want to live. Millennials don't want to be caged to a stringent office policy or be prevented from what they want to do and when they want to do it.

The issue here is, the younger generation is very selective about where they want to work. Is long-term employment a dead end then? For many of the younger generation, it appears to be. They don't want to see themselves enslaved to a single organization and not knowing how to take their career to the next level. For employers, they may have to grapple with newer and more creative ways to retain new hires for as long as they can.

What could be responsible for today's younger generation's attitude towards work? In a way, it can be attributed to the highly dynamic changes and instability in today's business climate. Imagine how many companies today get bought out or merge, leading to sometimes drastic changes to office policies, and not many millennials will be able to accommodate the situation.

So, this makes the concept of long-term employment a kind of an aberration to this generation of workers. There is so much going on in the world of business, many innovations and new companies are springing up to give the younger generation a lot of opportunities, with many companies seeking creative and dynamic talents to join their company. Employers just have to find a way around the situation.

Should employers avoid hiring the younger generation employees then? This will be a hard decision to make for any employer. Clearly, to the employer, the gig economy has its disadvantages because many workers that would be found in the freelancing sector are those who are not willing to stay longer on a job.

The Pros and Cons of Gig workers for Businesses

It can be a win-win situation for employers when they decide on the gig working option, but leaders should also remain aware of the risks in hiring this way. Employers can use the sector to boost their productivity, but at the same time, it can be the reason why a department fails in its duties. As executives are mindful of the pros associated with the gig economy, they should also take note that there are cons as well.

Pros

It Is Inexpensive

Hiring gig workers on the other side of the world when the option presents itself is quite inexpensive compared to paying long-term in-house staff. They do not need to worry about onboarding, requiring an office, or even providing tools for the freelancer to work with. Because companies don't have to pay for medical, retirement, and health insurance benefits for freelancers, the choice of gig workers for employers, therefore, fits well in terms of saving costs.

Access to a Pool of Unique Workers

Employers will find workers of different expertise, ages, and experience level to choose from. Leaders will find workers at the expert level, the middle level, and the entry-level depending on the nature of the task that needs to be done. Also, the flexibility in their operation can be a feature for employers to capitalize on. When hiring workers in other time zones, jobs that need quick attention can be contracted out and be ready on the manager's desk the next morning.

Good for Startups to Quickly Scale Up

Startups may not have enough facilities to scale up their businesses quickly. Contracting of gig workers can help in this area. Small businesses that are looking to grow their businesses should see the gig workers as needed to reach their target goals in the shortest possible time. I know a handful of small-business owners who use gig workers frequently to grow their business. The difficulty --- especially at first --- is usually the time it takes to find a suitable freelancer for the job, but it is well worth the effort, especially when looking for a gig worker that will go for a long-term assignment.

Lower Burden of Risk

Employers enjoy the benefit of little to no risk when hiring gig workers, because gig workers are not regular employees. This makes termination of the contract much more manageable when things don't work out as expected in the work contract.

Cons

Alongside the positives of the growth of the gig economy, in terms of effectiveness for companies and other advantages attached to the system, there are also some disadvantages.

Proficiency Issue

One prominent downside with gig workers is the proficiency issue. Having a large pool of potential workers to pick from has both good and bad in it. It's a mix of low-experience workers with limited skills and experienced experts. Quality delivery is a concern. It is commonplace to find gig workers take up jobs they are not trained on or are experienced enough to handle. Sometimes quality is affected when these contractors are working at a faster rate than really necessary. Working to beat the deadline is another reason why gig workers fail to deliver quality work.

Availability Uncertainty

Employers will have to ensure gig workers are free to meet their schedules and deadlines. Devising a 'Plan B' as a backup can be the saving grace. Better still, employing a team of gig workers can do the trick for company leaders looking to hire from that sector.

Inability to Build a Strong Relationship

In a typical working environment, building relationships is, of course, recommended and encouraged. This is because regular employees relate to the goings-on in the company; they are familiar with the company culture. With gig workers, the story is different; it is difficult to build such relationships. Freelancers maybe have more than a single client to deal with, and so may find committing to an individual client a relatively rare possibility.

This may not apply to all countries. Gig workers may help to keep the headcount of a company's workforce down, but there can be a twist to it. How much control employers have over gig workers will determine what class of worker classification they will be placed --- even if they work as freelancers. Employers will have to defend their claim to a gig worker when contacted for an audit by governmental and regulatory bodies.

Employers must take great care in this issue because of possible serious repercussions. An important guideline to adhere to is that for a worker to be classified as a gig worker, such workers usually must have full control over their business and not the hiring company. They should be in complete control of when to work, how they will complete the job task or assignment, and the charges they place on clients.

There is no arguing that the gig economy has now become of the ever-changing business climate. While the different players enjoy some advantages, they as well suffer some disadvantages as highlighted above. Perhaps, company executives working on in-house employee benefits can eliminate the need for outside contract workers. Will changing employee benefits do the trick for employers? Let´s discuss it in the next chapter.

CHAPTER FIVE

Benefits Impact

One potent tool in the hands of employers to attract potential talents to join their workforce and retain existing ones for much longer is employee benefits.

Employee benefits are the non-monetary compensation an employer offers employees. The benefits are significant parts of an employment contract. Looking at things from the direction of work-life patterns embraced by the younger generations, the benefits a job offers above the average remuneration makes a lot of difference to avoid high turnover in an organization.

The impact of benefits on the employee should be significant to the employer to pay more attention to. From the employee's angle, the benefits help their work life and the general well-being of their family and theirs. To the employer, they help staff retention, improve performance, and make the employee happy. Owing to the competition to attract the best talent to a company, the benefits an employer gives over salary has a lot more positive effects than can be imagined.

Employees place a high priority on benefits. Various reports attest to this. The Aflac survey of 2016 reported that 60 percent of employees would be more willing to apply for jobs with lower pay if they come with better benefits. Also, in the survey, 42 percent of respondents said a continuous improvement on benefits is one responsibility employers can embark on to retain workers. 16% of the participants reported that they have turned down an offer or have left their current employment on the bases of unattractive benefits in the past year.

Employers should see benefits beyond just making their in-house workers happy; it goes far above that. If leaders know how it robs on their company branding, they will do everything on their part to make this aspect of employee welfare one that prospects will find difficult to resist. It should be stated that talents intending to send in an application most times will look at the benefits package before applying to a company or only accept an offer after thoroughly examining what the benefits package entails.

Types of Benefits for Employees

It is a kind of battlefield between companies on who has the best benefits package to attract talents to the company. Since employers know the priority of finding the right fit for their vacant positions, they will be more committed to offering the most benefits as their best-selling point to bring the needed recruit into the company. Leaders who desire to win over the best available workers in the labor market for their company cannot but put out a benefit that beats every other one around. That is the only way right now to have the best workers to join a company.

There is nothing an organization can do besides that because employees are also on the lookout for the best place that makes them comfortable.

It is challenging to say most companies offer benefits. One cannot take away the edge companies that give the most benefits have over others that don't. The advice I give is for leaders to provide more attention to those benefits with the highest value to potential employees if they are not going to offer a huge list.

But what benefits attract potential talents and existing employees the most? It's worth finding out.

The Most Attractive Benefits to Employees

Clearly, health benefits rank among the most attractive benefits for employees. The reason is obvious. Health is wealth; nothing works when health is affected. Every employee not only wants to maintain perfect health but also for their families. It is already known that employees always prioritize health benefits because of the cost and the need to stay healthy, making this benefit the biggest attraction for workers.

In the Aflac survey mentioned earlier, another important finding was that 55 percent of respondents said health insurance happens to be one of the most valued benefits that impact their satisfaction on the job. It contributes significantly to retaining and attracting new talents from the labor market --- even among younger employees.

Retirement Benefits

No one knows what the future holds, so people are admonished to prepare for an uncertain future through savings. No matter how young one is today, they won't be young forever. A time comes when old age comes calling, and working as before is no longer attainable.

The future is the focus here with the retirement benefit, making it a crucial one that attracts employees to want to stay with a company. 'Retire well' is a slogan on the lips of many people today, and the media is making the need to plan for retirement a necessity. Statistics show that retirement benefits are growing to be one of the most attractive benefits to employees and a primary reason why they will choose to work with a company when the retirement package is right.

Transportation Benefits

Transportation benefits are very valuable to employees, especially in regions where traffic can be hectic. In a recent US Environmental Protection Agency report, workers in companies where the employer prioritizes reducing stress and cost expended on commuting find their companies to be a very attractive place to work. They get more workers willing to stay longer.

The record is staggering, as 86% of the American workforce view commuter benefits as useful and beneficial to determining their choice of a place to work. These benefits can come in the form of parking benefits, transit passes, ride-sharing boards, and reimbursements on charges for public transportation. It all depends on what individual companies are offering. Traveling in official company cars can be another motivation for the younger generation. This is an incentive that applies to most prominent corporations. If a company car is attached to a job offer, depending on the region under consideration, most employees love this benefit.

Education Benefits

About one-third of employees stated that educational benefits from their employer are crucial to getting the desired satisfaction from their job. The most common employees in this category are younger people, women, and those who have reached a certain degree of educational level.[18]

Employees want to upgrade their educational status while working and will jump at the opportunity to work with organizations giving them this privilege. Employees know that advancing their education offers them a higher advantage, and places them in good standing to go for more senior positions and better earnings.

The education benefits that are most important here are tuition reimbursement programs and job training that is fully paid for by the company.

The value of educational benefits and its role in retention and employee recruitment has been on the increase in recent years.

Employers need not be told to improve educational benefits, because like health benefits, continuously working to improve the benefits helps retain loyal employees in the company. As seen in the earlier chapters of this book, employers should not fret about losing their employees after training them.

Vacation Benefits

Vacation benefits are always attractive. Employees ease their inner tensions and stress and find it an opportunity to see the world, make friends, and expand their networks.

It's not all work and no play --- there is more to life. Going on vacation and visiting places helps one's mental health. The younger generations want to visit new places and meet new people. Employers that have a benefits package that enables workers to travel and escape from office pressures are happier for this. And this benefit is not all about the employee. Vacations help employees to be more productive overall. They come back refreshed and prepared to approach tasks well energized, with improved performance.

In recent times, employers now offer less traditional benefits. The focus goes far beyond employees' work-life --- it covers their entire life, including that of their family. Benefits such as free childcare and gym membership subsidies are some more recent additions. But what is the advantage for the employer of offering these benefits?

Employee Loyalty Gets a Boost through Benefits

Employee loyalty is at stake without benefits. Of course, it's hardly possible for companies not to have any benefits alongside regular wages in this day and age. Companies that fail to attend to employee benefits should be ready to face the consequences. America, for instance, has an increasing workforce of employees that are not satisfied with their current job. What could be responsible for this can be traced back to sliding work ethics, and the lack of benefits employees are provided. Retaining such employees will always be a difficult one when there is a job opening elsewhere. The competitors become better for it.

Benefits in an organization should not be static. There should be constant improvement by employers. Benefits should be frequently reviewed to meet the current needs of employees. Employers should also communicate with their existing workers on how they feel about current benefits, and which ones they might want to add to the list. Even when the benefits that exist are not extremely popular, the employees can trust the company will make changes if communication is cordial between the two.

The impact of benefits on the employee foster greater engagement --- giving satisfaction and enhancing productivity. The more and better benefits an employer makes available to its workers, the more their employees are likely to stay in the organization for a more extended period.

The drive is all about improving employee commitment and encouraging efficiency, which other tools like gamification helps to Provide. That will be our next topic.

CHAPTER SIX

How Gamification Can Increase Motivation

The traditional workplace is the officious environment where the atmosphere is filled with serious-looking individuals. The approach to work takes a rigid form and offers somewhat dull routines. What would it be like if employees are given the freedom to carry out their tasks in a playstyle with everybody enjoying themselves, having fun as if in an entertainment arena?

Every employee likes a stress-free environment to work, and when the job is performed in a playful environment, one can rest assured employees --- especially the younger generation and millennials --- will love every bit of it. It is no longer a world of that formal, stern-looking, and rigid composure that rules in today's work environment. Innovation and the principle of games are finding a place in offices.

Gamification in Brief

Consider gamification as a derivation from games, and one won't be too far off. It is a term that borrows its application from the gaming world. It is not the standard games we are referring to here but work activities in the office.

Gamification is the use of the general game concept in the workplace. Since human nature likes an environment that is relaxed and fun-filled, gamification capitalizes on this to drive engagement and improve employees' performance. The elements of game-playing such as competitiveness, commitment to high achievement, and to be quickly awarded for the performance are enshrined in the gamification design.

Comparing these principles closely to games, gamification gets employees engaged. It encourages them to strive to outperform one another in a competitive but fun sort of atmosphere.

Gamification of corporate culture can assist the company's culture through various initiatives and programs. It can aid employees to discover ways to participate in shaping their corporate culture. It can also make business data and its values more available.

Gamification is all about increasing engagement using a digital environment to assist staff in achieving specific goals. The worker performs a game that provides points, status, and benefits as they enhance the company's abilities, goals, or objectives, with the theory being that we all like to compete and engage in friendly contests.

With the increasing use of social media, mobile apps, and the complexity of mobile technology, individuals are more linked and play games more than ever. Gamification naturally fits in many workers ' worlds. It can make workers and their tasks enjoyable and available, resulting in employees being more involved and productive.

It seeks to help employees carry out their tasks in a way using aspects of games such as play, challenge, and fun. Like games, it takes the game-style mechanism, structure, and reward system into designing a process that makes the worker take a different approach to get problems solved in the office, flexibility, and creativity are encouraged.

There is usually a motive for the gamification adopted by an employer. The objective must be well spelled out. The employer would have seen a specific behavior in the workers that need to be corrected. The expectation must be there to be able to evaluate the results afterward.

Gamification is a method geared towards influencing the behaviors employers want in their employees. The art of gamification goes beyond merely rewarding employees with badges or points; it is driven by an excellent motive to encourage and influence specific behavioral characteristics that employers want in their staff. The practice is built on human psychology as well as behavioral science.

Core factors targeted by the practice are enhancing abilities and increasing employee motivation. To change employees' behavior and help them approach things differently, they need motivation, and this works along with the ability to carry out the practice.

Many internet users have used gamification one time or the other without really knowing. The typical case is when people are made to respond to a prompt and are rewarded for taking the needed action. This is a light form of the gamification process.

As a commonly used strategy in real-world applications, primarily online, this practice is introduced in the work environment to achieve company-set goals more effectively. The players here are employees and sometimes can involve customers depending on the platform it is deployed and the target. Gamification can span across the different departments of an organization.

Gamification is not merely making a game out of a work process. It is a development strategy that drives employees and enhances business outcomes using psychology. The application is designed in such a way to add motivational techniques and game mechanics to introduce competition to the work environment. It builds the behaviors in the employee to achieve such goals that businesses require to improve production and quality.

In a nutshell, gamification can help to:

- Optimize workflow
- Educate employees
- Engage employees
- Motivate employees
- Attract young talents

There is a growing trend in the application of gamification, and some positives have been recorded. In a recent Gallup survey, it was noted that there was better performance in companies that use gamification in their operation. The report also discovered less staff turnover of between 25% to 65 %, with 37% less absentee-ism.[19]

These are outstanding benefits to show that the practice is yielding fruitful results. I can affirm that the younger generation will love the use of gamification. There is no doubt that millennials will fancy working in an organization that applies this principle in their workplace. This is obvious because the generation we live in places so much attention to playing games and having fun even while working.

Components in the Gamification Set Up

Just as the physical gaming practice is developed with rules and tools, gamification has features that make it work most effectively. The set up comprises but is not limited to:

- Badges – they are awarded after achieving a particular goal.
- Leaderboards – indicates the current position of the participant, letting others know how things stand
- Levels – it points to the level of participation and leads the path to more tasks and achievements.
- Scores and points – points and scores are assigned for reaching a specified goal
- Challenges – this is geared towards competitiveness.
- Notification – lets users know and be encouraged when they carry out a particular action.

Essentially, the incentives offered should not be monetary, as this won't make any difference to the average work-life where wages and salaries are used. The issue is there must be a reward system for every achievement attained by the employee.

Different Kinds of Gamification

Leaders have the choice on which gamification method is best for their organization. There are many ways to treat the content in your organization when you're considering gamification, but a look at these two styles below will serve as a sufficient guide on the types of gamification that can be applied to motivate employees for better engagement.

1. Structural Gamification
2. Content Gamification

Structural Gamification

Structural gamification is used to 'gamify' a content. This type makes a game-like structure of the material. Here the content doesn't become the game; it is instead presented in a game-like manner. The original content structure remains unchanged. The characteristics of structural gamification are:

- The gamification template is usable in all kinds of training
- It requires only instruction design to make content more friendly for learning
- Drives engagement for compliance
- It is relatively easy to develop
- It is easy to move around

Content Gamification

Content gamification completely turns content into a game. It is designed specifically for a given content and can't be applied to other content. It is seen as a serious game template.

- Content gamification requires organization and content re-work
- It is only useable for the intended learning goals and not another
- Takes much longer to develop
- Applicable for new skill acquisition

Gamification and Its Impact

Gamification has an impact on both employees and employers. We will first look at a positive impact.

To comprehend why gamification is useful, we need to know how it works and probably why it has the impacts that it does. We also need to know the keys required to execute gamification in a company effectively.

To be fair, gamification is a social strategy. By this, it means participants in the system don't work alone; they interact with others in a competitive atmosphere. Working together in this way with achievements and reward system in place, employees are motivated to give their best and are happier for this at the workplace. It is a win-win situation for both employers and employees. The employer reaps the benefit of the employee output resulting from the motivation they receive to work better. Employees feel engaged and happier in their employment.

As companies focus on company goals, gamification can assist the workplace to be more productive and engaging.

Gamification changes commitment in a positive direction and therefore motivates employees to change their behavior towards their duties --- even going above and beyond expectations. Is gamification effective, and how well are companies embracing the technology?

Employers should get more jobs done efficiently when they make work more enjoyable. Gabe Zichermann, the author of the book "The Gamification Revolution," who is also the founder of Dopamine --- a consulting company centered on workers and consumers --- says that "When employers reward customers for having fun using simple events, they give their very best and contribute actively and constantly." [20] It is seen that gamification has a significant impact on both the customer and the employee. No wonder 55% of Americans say they are interested in working for a company that uses gamification in their business to increase staff efficiency.

Gamification has been very successful in motivating people to change their behavior, build skills, or solve problems. Thus, gamification has been efficient in motivating and engaging more employees. By using specific characteristics of true games, gamification has transformed many other operations into motivational games in companies.

Since the use of gamification relies on simplicity, employees are encouraged to work hard without feeling any added stress in the process. In the psychological field, gamification utilizes periodic favorable feedback, which may include points, scores, level badges, and advancement --- among others --- to motivate consumers.

It improves the perceived capacity of users by simplifying challenging assignments or difficulties through exercise. The motivation for people may be to receive a gift card, but what drives the practice is the recognition for participation with a given reward.

How Employees Use Gamification in the Workplace

Many companies' problems involve solving issues rigidly according to their company culture, which can prevent the free flow of information and skills. Change is affected, and business processes stay closed and are not growing as a result. However, there is increasing proof that individuals and behaviors will change, given the correct incentives. Perhaps surprisingly, such incentives need not be financial; other triggers can make for more efficiency and promote retention of employees and customers.

The following triggers should be considered in the context of gameplay strategy directed at enhancing engagement of employees:

- Employees' activities on the company's platform are the starting point for getting started with the gamification application.
- Employees should visit websites, including corporate blogs, news boards, and share corporate news in social networks. They can follow the company's social networking platform. They can also participate in surveys, comment on blogs, and forum posts.
- Employers must have the gamification software in a position to monitor and evaluate these actions, such as the amount of "Likes," amount of remarks, download numbers, among other activities performed by the employees.

However, employers should not restrict incentives to external benefits such as points, badges, and the like since they are rather one-dimensional. Employers should consider other motivations. It is essential to involve users well into the gamification design and to achieve the right balance between the external and intrinsic rewards mechanisms.

A Great Gamification Design

While gamification can become an essential component of the workplace, it needs to be administered correctly. Considering how challenging it is to create a hit game, I don't think it's surprising that constructing effective gamification in a work setting may not come that easy.

From the minimal errors that waste energy to large scale result-oriented ones that can turn customers on, the art needs the proper commitment to getting it right.

Some key points to consider in the planning process include:

- Employers should make sure they clearly state the objectives of their organization. This is a particularly significant move to note before getting into the advanced stage of development. It is better to know what is expected for the development from the onset.Executives should think about their corporate culture. They need to consider the kinds of incentives used to motivate staff and how leaders can develop an awareness program that connects well with society.
- The design should concentrate on which behaviors first to try to encourage or prevent as the case applies. It can adopt a dynamic approach. Changing the scheme of incentives regularly will guarantee that the employee is committed, stays involved, and is not bothered by the same choices.

- Employers should not "game" employees for whatever reason. Companies must design game systems that improve the time on the job rather than exploit their employees. As mentioned previously, never should cash be the motivating incentive --- it doesn't provide encouragement as one may suppose.
- Employee consent in the gamification process is essential. When executives use gamification to motivate and involve their employees, they should remember to have their employees' permission. To succeed, participation must be voluntary. They should be aware of what they are getting into beforehand.
- Fun is not experienced unless the employees consent to the game. Some variables of employees' approval must be present for gamification to boost motivation effectively. Employees must be aware of it, comprehend the laws of the game, and consider it fair.

Companies that want to enhance their personal training programs also see gamification as a means to increase commitment and friendly competition. It could be said that a desire to play, to fail, and try again is a core of what makes learning an attractive exercise. When performed well, gamification can be used to form congenial user interactions and drive individuals to go further; to construct learning strategies and to influence behavior.

Areas of Gamification Application

Customer Support

Applying gamification in the customer support department is aimed to encourage performance, quick attendance, and meeting customer satisfaction goals.

Excellent achievements and gamification incentives can encourage customer service agents to assist clients more efficiently. It also encourages employees to share new ideas and thoughts with other members of the team.

Gamification can increase sales. It rewards not only the final sale but also all the steps it takes to reach the final sale.

Marketing

Employers can encourage their employees to share social media info about the business. Employees are encouraged to be active participants on the social platforms of the company and help in the marketing drive for the company.

Product Development

Gamification can assist staff in finishing projects, working more closely together, and be more productive on a timely basis.

Other departments, such as the sales unit, administrative department, and others can all have gamification applied for efficiency.

When Gamification Doesn't Work as Expected

Employers want happy, committed staff. Customers are treated better, and productivity is more significant for employees who appreciate their job. But not all game-based apps have the same impact as do other great apps. Statistics on gamification are not always on the positive side; though it surpasses the negatives in more significant measures. Gartner estimates that the company goals may not be achieved by 80% of created workplace gamification apps because of bad design and a lack of creativity.[21]

Productivity suffers when the employees in a company are not adequately engaged. The explanation for this is simple. Workplace games won't be an instant fix for the company's low productivity. This might be due to the company culture. Companies can have adverse cultures and procedures that discourage employees. Other times, poor management harms productivity. Sometimes, an employee doesn't suit the job or fit in the company culture or team. An employee gamification app can not miraculously solve all these problems. Nevertheless, when expertly designed and applied, gamification psychology can and does have a beneficial effect on everyday workplace problems.

If gamification projects fail, they are often due to bad planning or implementation. Employees with low motivation will perceive the game as yet another set of duties to be performed in the workplace and would only play along just enough to hold on their positions. Most don't bother about the new gamification program, or only pay lip service to it. Or they could see it as a way to waste time. In contrast, more committed and loyal employees --- particularly those with a competitive mind --- could be tempted to sabotage peers or to cheat.

Another reason for gamification failure is the desire to overuse gamification in jobs. Just throwing a solution off the shelf at the personnel and trying to stay positive is not a sound methodology. This was demonstrated in a study conducted in 2013 by Omnicare, an American medical and pharmaceutical firm, now acquired by CVS Health.

A leaderboard was developed with monetary incentives for those who could finish up with their client calls as quickly as possible. The leaderboard was built to decrease the waiting time in the customer service department. Unfortunately, the initiative backfired with more time spent on receiving customer calls. This was because employees thought they were too closely supervised and probably had to spend enough time to assist customers. The result also was that some employees were leaving the establishment, with a high turnover being recorded. What went wrong here? Implementation and planning weren't done correctly. The results of this study should provide a lesson for employers. Employees should know why the gamification strategy was implemented, and they should agree with its purposes and objectives.

When performed correctly, gamification can produce impactful outcomes for employees across an organization. At its heart, gamification involves motivating individuals at an emotional level to attain their objectives. One way to motivate employees is to give them challenging and personalized problems, promote them to advance through the stages, and get them committed to their best performance mentally.

All this sounds very nice, but I highly suspect that implementers are focusing more on the technology and mechanical elements of gamification apps, rather than their prospective customers. Unlike how difficult it can be to understand humans, it is comparatively easy to understand technology fully.

Gamification is a great technique that improves productivity in similar ways as flexibility in the workplace enhances work-life balance. Overall, gamification is a good practice for employers to implement to encourage and get the best from their employees.

CHAPTER SEVEN

Ensuring Flexibility in Work-Life Balance

Work-life balance has a lot to do with the general well-being of the employee in an organization. Employers cannot be less concerned about it because it determines how well the employee will engage with the company and perform the duties assigned. The topic of work-life balance is crucial to workers. Some employees have families or other issues in their private lives away from work that requires their attention. Flexibility in work-life balance will take care of this.

The balance is a way of putting a measure of control and freedom in the hands of the employee in terms of work schedules, timing, and approach. Work-life flexibility answers the question of how many days an employee will choose to work, and for how long?

Flexibility allows employees to work longer hours to cut down on the number of days in the week to work. In the end, the worker still ends up spending the required number of working hours for the week but in a lesser number of days. It enables the employee to decide when to clock in and clock out. Working remotely is not exempted from this; depending on the role the employee plays in the office, the option of working remotely on some days of the week is a possibility when work-life balance is enabled.

It's a big thumbs up to an employer who sees value in an employee's work-life balance by enabling a flexible work pattern. To have the best output in their employees, executives cannot neglect creating an atmosphere where the employee is comfortable working for the organization. The workers' life within and outside of the company should interest leaders.

A company that values the lives of workers outside of work is likely to experience low turnover and have a highly productive workforce. How a business can help its employees in job flexibility is a challenge that employers should take time to work on. It is essential to find the best way for an employee to achieve a maximum level of efficiency and a suitable work-life balance.

How does a business allow flexibility in its workplace to have a positive work-life balance for employees? Although it is not only the employer's sole duty to balance work and life, it helps in many areas in the employee's work-life, including productivity, encouragement, job satisfaction, and optimal performance.

Both the worker and the employer benefit from providing their staff with more flexibility in the performance of their duties. By enabling a bit more flexibility in the work environment, a business can expect to get the very best from the employee. Never should employers think being hard and strict on work patterns is the best way to have control over a business --- it really doesn't work that way. It takes two to tango; there must be a mutual understanding between employer and employee.

Understanding how business and an individual can use a flexible approach to achieve better work-life balance can also lead to the needed positive change in the company. Indeed, having a balance between work and life has benefits that many people wouldn't realize.

The Benefits

If an employer is flexible in working hours, where the job is performed, and how it is completed, then the employee-employer relationship will be cordial and helps the company to grow. The trust factor is what comes into play here. Both parties will operate in openness.

Since retention of employees is a problem for some employers, a measure of flexibility is often helpful in alleviating this issue. First of all, employers can allow part-time positions as well as full-time. This not only provides flexibility in scheduling but also reduces costs expended on employees. It should be up to the employee to ensure that part-time is the right fit for the personal economy but also a fit for the employer who works hard to provide full-time jobs.

A company could also reap excellent benefits by enabling employees to go by their own schedules rather than the typical 9 - 5 schedule. By being flexible rather than just telling employees when to work, employees can better coordinate their lives outside the workplace. Although it depends on the sector, individual employers can enable their employees to operate by the timetable that works best for then. It breeds commitment, job satisfaction, and ensures better productivity.

The option to work from home is another popular privilege in a company. Employees with this degree of flexibility often work wherever they want, from a home office or even when traveling around the globe. The integration of these elements of job flexibility enables workers to create a stronger feeling of work-life stability.

A given timetable may ensure that a parent can pick up children from school. Whatever flexibility does for the life of workers outside the workplace is essential for the total balance.

If finding a balance between work and life needs the application of flexibility on the part of employers, how does an organization give it? As stated earlier, the turnover of employees would be much smaller if the employer provides more flexibility. This leads to happier employees, who often develop a feeling of loyalty to the company. This loyalty implies not only that employees would want to stay, but also that they do their utmost best. Productivity rates go through the ceiling, sick days are less frequent, and stress is dramatically lowered.

When workers are more aware of their ownership and control of their own life, they tend to have stronger interactions with the leadership of an organization. A balanced work-life tend to be more motivated and less stressed at the job, increasing their productivity and reducing employees ' conflict in the workplace.

Companies with a reputation for promoting work-life equilibrium are very appealing to potential employees and will attract a precious pool of applicants for new jobs. They also tend to have higher retention rates, leading to less time-consuming training, greater allegiance to the company, and a higher level of in-house knowledge. Studies have shown that workers with a favorable balance work better, so it is highly valuable for leaders and businesses to promote this.

Cutting Down on Stress

Research reveals that flexible working arrangements can decrease stress because workers are happy with their employment, live better, and have a healthy work-family balance. Overall, employees with a strong work-life balance align far better than those who do not in the workplace. They are more involved and less likely to seek another job elsewhere in years to come. They enjoy better general health, improved mental health, and less stress. Participating in flex-time agreements encourages employees to understand that they get the discretion to fit jobs into their life, and that helps to reduce the stress associated with the conventional work-life.

Research conducted on more than 19,000 employees in nine different businesses, including pharmaceutical, production, financial, and professional services, showed that stress and burnout among employees involved in flexible working arrangements were smaller. Similarly, research by the staff of a big multinational corporation discovered that higher flexibility was linked to improved health: less reported stress and anxiety and better physical health. [22] There are few things for experts to do about stress, and because it can lead to more severe problems, the reduction of employee stress should be a priority for employers.

Giving flexibility in the workplace or allowing flexible work hours can go a long way toward guaranteeing that workers are stress-free. This is because if employees have a flexible working timetable, they will discover better job satisfaction and a better balance between work and life.

Builds Trust

Confidence is something gained and not granted. Whether this is a higher commitment of employees to their role, better employee satisfaction, or enhanced workplace development and progress, employees get more confident in their jobs.

Flexible arrangements in the workplace benefit all concerned. When an individual feels confident, no matter on which side it is, there is this feeling of convenience. Their sense of private accountability improves their productivity.

Balancing

A healthy work-life balance may be one of the employee's most potent resources. It is invaluable to allow them to separate between work, life, and family. This means they should think about the job at work, and what they want in their free periods should not be disrupted by their work.

Employers can promote this. A favorable balance between work and times outside of work can be accomplished by carefully shaping an employee's agreement or the strategy to align with the office culture. The promotion of an excellent work/life equilibrium through workplace flexibility guarantees personal growth. This should be crucial to the employer because it reduces stress, helps work readiness, and serves as a potential for enhanced productivity.

In other research that studies the connection between flexible working routines and balance, workers with flexible work schedules showed considerably higher work-life balance rates than their counterparts using traditional fixed-time schedules. For many employees in offices, the perceived usability and accessibility of these job plans seems to be the main component in attaining stability in the workplace.

Increase Work/Family Balance

An advantage of work-life balance is that it builds a good relationship between the family and the employee. The steadiness between job and family has two dimensions: job involvement with family, and work interference. Job and workplace characteristics can have a beneficial or detrimental impact on family life, while elements of an employee's family position can impact employee performance and behaviors towards employment. A stable work arrangement can contribute to maximizing the balance between work and the family, which benefits employees and employers alike.

The latest research on the impacts of the accessibility of flexible schedules on the interface between job and family revealed that flexible schedules had decreased conflict between females in the workplace, but not for males. Scheduling flexibility enabled employees to minimize family conflicts, promote work-family relationships, and to improve work and performance in the workplace and at home.

Research of executives in five countries' workplaces shows that workers operating in a setting that is more family-friendly have a reduced level of family-work conflict. In turn, reduced friction between the workplace and family was linked to higher job satisfaction.

If the opportunity to chat with other staff on the business culture occurs, discussing matters such as how family-friendly the company is etc., the effort is well worth it to employers. If questions such as, are there any advantages to daycare? Is there time off for emergencies— a feeling of empathy for parents? They can be answered in the affirmative; then, the company is sure to attract more potential employees.

By observing the environment, the attitude, the behavior, and the sociability of employees, one can get to know how flexible the leadership is. Studies by the Columbia University National Center on Addiction and Substance Abuse say that teenagers that participate in family meals frequently (5-7 times a week) report having more significant links with their parents/caregivers. Instead of letting TV, YouTube, or computer games fill the night, scheduling family time together before bed helps to build a bond.[23] This strengthening of family bonds is made possible by flexibility at work and creating adequate balance.

Other balancing techniques are bringing kids --- when and if one can --- to work. They get to understand and bond well with parents that way. This helps them to realize that they are valued both at work and at home.
It is important to know that balance implies excellent time management abilities for everybody. For an employer to enable flexibility for their workers, mutual trust is essential.

Helps Mental and Physical Well-Being

The results of numerous research studies indicate that flexibility in working habits provide the employee with more choice or control, and can have a beneficial impact on the health and well-being of employees. For instance, workers at extended-care centers have shown that if employees enjoy flexibility, they will engage in healthier behavior and probably lower adverse health outcomes such as sickness, absenteeism, stress, and other work-related hazards. Studies of overtime work, flex-time, and fixed-term agreements did not show any crucial impacts on physical, mental, or general health or any of the wellness results examined.

CHAPTER EIGHT

Trust in the Workplace: A Criteria for Productivity

Trust has never been anything less than necessary in our everyday life as humans. The same applies to the corporate world. The workplace cannot do without this attribute. Trust is reciprocal; people get to trust those who have trust in them.

Trust is a strong virtue, a personal attribute that portrays one's character in a good light. Employers and employees ought to demonstrate trust to make the workplace an interesting one with the positive outcome of increasing productivity.

Moreover, employees will not operate efficiently if they don't trust their leaders. Distrust is what births the conventional eye-service paradigm that takes root in an environment where this virtue is missing. Lack of trust in the workplace does not help a company grow.

The employee will be unwilling to make decisions when they know the right thing to do but will instead seek permission for every small thing. They will not go the extra mile if they don't know if others will support them. Lack of trust lets workers operate in secrecy. Leaders will be afraid to let employees know about adverse developments in the company, so issues don't get resolved easily. They will opt to stay silent instead of addressing them quickly. If employers think employees will not support their ideas or appreciate their thoughts, they will be less likely to come out in the open all the time.

In the words of Amanda Setili, President of Setili & Associates --- a strategic consulting firm, with many prominent clients such as Coca-Cola, Delta Airlines and UPS: "Trust is when people think they can trust others to do what they have told them to do." Setili holds trust as a major necessity for employers and employees to make things move on in the organization as desired. I can't but agree as well that trust is about openness in the workplace.

Trustworthy executives can bring excellent benefits to an organization, including increased commitment, innovation, and productivity for its employees. Employers are much more likely to get innovative ideas and strategies from their workers when trust rules because freedom comes with trust. Trust also allows individuals to affect others, which is crucial not only for leaders but for employees at all levels.

Many studies from the Great Place To Work Institute and elsewhere have demonstrated that businesses with high-trust cultures are more successful financially than those that are not.

Indeed, it is an expensive thing not to have trust among employees in an organization, says David Horsager, CEO of the Trust Edge Leadership Institute in St. Paul, Minn. This author opines that each problem that leaders believe they have --- whether it's a management issue, a marketing issue, a commitment problem, or some other issue --- has its root in lack of trust and trust among staff. Of the 1,202 working-class adults who were surveyed in the Autumn of 2018, 21 percent said they would work for longer hours if they trusted their leaders, according to the Trust Outlook 2018. One third stated that if its employers kept their commitments, they would remain with an employer longer, and 28% said they would increase their tenure if transparency were practiced at all levels.[24] Everything points to the fact that trust is crucial in the workplace. Employee retention depends on it to a large extent. There can be no mutual understanding between parties without it.

One of the main variables to consider is the problem of job performance in an organization that relies on the feeling of trust. Trust is the foundation of all healthy relations and interactions. In professional communications, it is as essential as in private interactions. A firm that has a solid feeling of trust in the workplace can better cope with the turbulence caused by competition and have a more unobstructed view of what the business stands for. The company with a trusted workforce can see the future realistically and optimistically.

Why Trust in the Workplace Matters

A recent study indicates that employees who feel confident that their employer allows them to manage how they work by themselves can increase their productivity rates. The survey carried out by Peldon Rose says that UK employees rate employers and colleagues' trust and autonomy as increasingly significant to keep them productive and satisfied in their workplace. But the study also demonstrates that many employers do not provide the funds and help they need to handle their workload. Although most of the people, 59%, say they function most productively at the office. A third, 33%, would like to see themselves given the freedom to handle how and when they choose to work; and 42% say their office does not promote a culture that enables them to function flexibly. Despite the evident importance of trust and autonomy that employees place on the job, employers tend to ignore this call, as concluded in the report.

According to other studies and surveys, 19% do not feel that their business trusts them. In similar studies, 42% of staff say their existing business environment does not have beneficial effects on their satisfaction, and only 36% appreciate their daily job.[25]

The survey revealed that while the workers recognize what makes them more efficient, they are seldom included in office decision making. Fifty-two percent of workers said they are not involved in planned office environment changes; 50 percent said they were not asked about office satisfaction, and 49 percent are not asked how efficiently the office is used. This indicates that employee involvement in business, long-term strategy, and the office atmosphere goes to show that workers know the motive behind choices and feel they should be consulted in the process. This will help motivate and retain employees.

Three Core Reasons Why Trust Matters

It is clear from the above that trust enhances productivity and fosters communication and liberty among employees and the employer. There are yet other vital reasons to have trust in an organization that looks to succeed.

1. Boosts Employee Engagement

Having trust in employees increases engagement and makes them more appreciated to get more involved in their job. This is a plus since every company requires a dedicated workforce to succeed. This will also encourage a higher feeling of employee satisfaction and a reduced turnover rate for employees.

2. Enables Flexible Work-Life Implementation

Flexible working time --- including part-time, early or later start-up time or work at home --- can enhance staff satisfaction. It can boost stability and boost the efficiency of the organization. It will improve employee retention and fight against burnout in the workplace.

3. Fosters Team Spirit

Trust builds team spirit. Findings show that employees are more comfortable in themselves and with each other in an environment with a high level of trust. Also, they are more open to working with others and taking prudent risks. Since they know that they don't have to look nervously over their shoulders, they instead can look at each other. In an atmosphere of trust, when they make a mistake, they know that they have a supportive team around them and that mistakes are a way to learn and develop.

How to Build Trust as an Employer

Trust is built by action or behavior and not by words. As a manager or leader in an organization, it doesn't make sense to simply say one should "trust" a specific worker or team; it must be demonstrated through daily behavior. Employers must show they trust their workers by entrusting roles in their hands and even tasks that seem difficult.

Executives should allow teams to make choices and create their ideas that will profit the company. Openness and transparency concerning critical decisions and business processes are related to employees as a mark of trust in the organization. Every employee in a team --- even though they play different roles --- should be treated equally. Never should leaders treat anybody or any team more positively than others.

Take Stock

Leaders should see what trust level exists between them and their employees. They should take a look at their behavior, too; it is a necessary step to evaluate the trust level that exists in the company. Do their teams exhibit trust?

The following seven questions should guide leaders to take proper stock of the trust level exhibited by employees in the organization:

Do leaders demonstrate to their staff that they care about their welfare?

Do leaders demonstrate they believe that their employees can do the job for which they are employed?

Do they influence employees on the things that most affect their job?

Do leaders allow employees to take part in decision making in their job?

Are leaders encouraging their workers to take risks?

Do employers stand by their words and express the same when it comes to showing trust in their workers?

Give Up Control

For employers to show they trust their workers, they must give up control to whoever is in the position to direct affairs. Managers need to delegate tasks appropriately, grant resources, and give a freehand for employees. Ceding control also needs some error tolerance. Instead of taking severe corrective actions, treat errors by employees as part of the learning curve. When employers empower employees, it breeds trust throughout the organization. Employees want to understand what is happening and want their voices to be heard.

Employers ought to re-evaluate the culture of the business if it does not offer some control to staff. Is the culture of the workplace encouraging feedback and input from all employees? How frequently does management interact with staff about modifications in the organization?

Empowering staff with more information creates opportunities for mutual action. When employees are in the decision-making circle, they feel confident that they have a voice in the business. As such, involvement in the scheduling process becomes more straightforward and management more effortless.

Sharing Information

Another meaningful way for leaders to take risks and demonstrate trust is to develop open and honest communication with their employees. Managers often refuse to communicate info and clarify their choices because of fears of early leaks or disagreement. Being transparent --- even under challenging conditions --- demonstrates that employers feel they can trust their employees with the truth. But employers should always carefully consider how and when to share vital information with their staff.

This challenge has been faced by a public sector manager for several years when making pay decisions with a continually decreasing budget. The arrived-at solution was to give a detailed description of the budgetary constraints and the use of merit criteria in this case. This detailed explanation of merit options worked quite well because the communication was effective. Such openness did not only prevent suspicions of partiality among employees, but it also demonstrated that the manager could entrust sensitive data to staff.

Go for the Necessary Change

Businesses should be prepared to take risks. This means employers should be ready to make changes in the organization of the company to accommodate trust in their establishment. Changes in the approach to work, and enabling a good measure of flexibility among other necessary changes should help to build confidence in the company.

Investment in Growth of Employees

Letting employees know that a company is prepared to invest in their potential and promote them, communicates trust to them. Leaders should endeavor to understand their employees and what their ambitions are for their careers, and then assist them in achieving their objectives. Employees are more likely to trust an organization when they know that the company is committed to the advancement and growth of its workforce.

CHAPTER NINE

Coaching Leadership

Leaders today are seeking autonomous employees, individuals who desire and are competent to assume responsibility for their work --- individuals who relate with the objectives and goals of the department and organization and have the preference to develop themselves for performing effectively. This vision of the status of employees is the cause of a change in the approach to thinking regarding leadership. The notion that better employees are those who do what is asked of them has been replaced with the mindset that better employees give direction to their own life, to the work they do in that life and are self-directed. Employees like this take full responsibility for the work they perform and the selections they make throughout the framework that is set by the company.

A forward-thinking leader will assist their employees to adopt a more self-directed attitude and give up some control to their staff. It is the difference between what the employees need for achieving their goals throughout the organization and how leaders can make sure the objectives are met. To be precise, the role of the leader changes --- to become a coaching leader as compared to an executive who allocates tasks. But what are the differences between the two?

The coach's objective is to enhance the performances as well as the learning opportunities of the employees. A leader can increase the self-directing potential of employees by becoming more of a coach. The fundamental objective is to show more confidence in the individual being coached. The coaching leadership mindset is:

- Seeking out employees with future potential rather than focusing on past performance.
- Encouraging employees to learn and to keep on learning.
- Freeing up individuals so they can perform to the best of their skills.
- A type of leadership that is the alternative to controlling and commanding.

There are several behavioral attributes, which are achieved by excellent leaders.

Self-Directing Promoted by Leaders

Leaders care that their employees give more direction to their life-work and stimulate them on autonomy. This is not always easy, as individuals being coached are more used to being reliant on their supervisors and managers, going to the leader with problems, and asking for permission. It is sometimes very tempting for leaders to advise and manage, but it will hinder growth towards self-direction by doing this.

Good Leaders Work from an Accepting Attitude

Employees must accept themselves with all their limitations and areas that need to be strengthened. This allows for the attitude of the leader to be more supportive concerning the employee. The foundation of good coaching is to accept the person who is being coached and the situation. Coaching is essential for the learning process to continue for the employees.

Good Leaders Are Transparent and Selectively Authentic

Coaching leaders are open to their staff with their intentions; regarding the reasons for the selection of this methodology, and regarding the background of any questions. Leaders also are open to what they experience throughout coaching, regarding their weaknesses and possible blind spots. This does not mean that leaders insinuate everything they feel and believe in conversations with those being coached. Good coaching involves making appropriate choices in what they say to those being coached regarding their ideas and emotions. Coaching leaders must make the choices that will most assist the employees being coached.

Good Leaders Have Trust in the Ability of Their Employees

In principle, people are competent to lead and give directions to others, as well as making the best decisions for themselves. Frequently, employees being coached are not aware of emotions like grief, entrepreneurship, disappointment, anger, and enthusiasm. The last thing that employees who are unaware of their feelings might want to do is to insert them into a discussion with the coach/leader. A lot of talent and abilities are wasted in these situations.

A good leader will help to exclude those blockades and to clear the way for unidentified and unused work and personality strengths and skills. The employee who is being correctly coached learns how to tap into these skills that they have not usually used, even if doing so is sometimes unpleasant and uncomfortable initially.

Good Leaders Communicate

Indeed, coaching leadership works toward achieving goals that have been created in advance and towards pre-set consequences. But a good leader is aware also that the path along which the objective is reached is just as essential. Questions such as how we shall communicate during coaching and how do we perform together in this process are used by leaders to assist their employees in learning. Leaders do not need to lean on their own preparation when the current situation requires something unique and different. To be precise, they can merge both the process and the goal.

Coaching Leaders Can Focus on Their Own Behavior

Self-directing is a long-lasting procedure that is not ended at any particular moment. Savvy leaders are aware of this fact and recognize the importance of some self-examination. They should consider questions such as, what is my attitude towards this individual who is being coached? What about my own fears, longings, and aversions? What role am I playing in the situation when conversations with a particular individual are so unpleasant? What do I evoke? What am I avoiding? Leaders make use of this self-determination and self-examination for adjusting the coaching platform where needed while stimulating self-reflection in the employee being coached.

Good Leaders Can Define Limits

Leaders are not always agreeing with their employees, but rather are aware of limits. Leaders are not afraid to challenge their employees; to place a mirror before the employee where essential. They are also mindful of the boundaries of their own abilities. A coaching leader is not a psychotherapist, and so they may not know what questions do or do not belong with the coaching of a particular individual. A leader, in this case, refers to another expert, if required.

Developing Employees

Leaders wish to bring employees from a low development level to a high development level. The raising of the competency level of an employee does not just occur overnight; it advances in slow steps. Leaders should not anticipate massive changes from one day to the next, especially if the employee is beginning at a low achievement level.

The best tactic is to state tasks and targets as clearly as possible during the coaching phase. It is vital to give a compliment as soon as employees demonstrate the preferred behavior at the time of executing a task they have been assigned. Leaders can then encourage them to complete their assignments independently once the leaders see that they have mastered the task.

The leader as a coach has three methods to support employee development:

- Reprimanding or correcting, if an employee has not performed a task appropriately. This is merely used when the leader is sure that the individual can eventually succeed with the job.
- Set targets and tasks that are clearly defined and instruct if needed.
- Give compliments or show appreciation if duties are performed appropriately, bringing about upsurge self-respect and self-confidence for the employee

These three methods are also termed as the fundamental skills of coaching. These foundational skills are an essential tool for effectiveness, next to a flexible approach to handle several leadership styles.

The situational leadership model has the hallmark of using the attitude of the employee as an initial point. It operates on the assumption that leaders, more or less direct employee's tasks all the time, but this could look different in different situations.

Here, the majority of the employees have set assignments that are performed autonomously, ones that the leader does not have to micro-manage.

A coaching leader will always work mutually with the employee and leave the accountability with the employee. A proactive leader will explain what the employee must modify and improve and then convince the employee of this.

Delegating

Some leaders find it hard to let go of tasks, and if this is the case, they should consider delegating. The most significant barrier to good rapport between employer and employee is the trust-control problem, as stated in an earlier chapter of this book. Delegating consists of a minimal amount of direct control, and by displaying a large amount of trust that an employee will achieve the assignment or task as they should. A leader cannot enforce a lot of control and anticipate the employee to function autonomously at the same time.

Nevertheless, the leader is accountable for everything that occurs in the realm of responsibility, and that is where resistance appears. Many leaders find this complicated and do not delegate --- or do not delegate appropriately --- for this very reason. However, delegating is also an essential aspect of being an effective leader.
Delegating tasks has specific benefits. The benefits for leaders are fewer direct management responsibilities and tasks, lowering the pressure of work, and having more time to dedicate to those activities that should not be delegated. The benefits for employees are that their commitment and support will be affirmed, and their autonomy and sense of responsibility will be escalated. They will also create new skills and competencies for additional professional development.

There are also advantages for the company. Delegating leads to higher availability and flexibility if it is implemented. The potential for more significant expertise on the unit floor will be created. Better decisions will be made, as the employee who makes the decisions will have achieved a better understanding of the situation and its effects on goals and targets. The limitations of the organizations will be mitigated, and the overall sense of responsibility will be increased.

Finally, there will be a higher volume of work done, as the workload will be better distributed between the employer and the employees.

Intervention Styles

Intervention style is a phrase used for explaining the behavior that coaching leaders use in their conversations with their employees. Leaders must identify that the different methods have several results. Every association between the leader and the employee has an influence. Every style used affects the relationship between employer and employee. Which intervention style will become most apparent, depending on the stage of the coaching style, the problem of an employee; or the situation and on how a leader evaluates that situation.

Leaders will have a specific style in which they feel at home as a coaching leader. Indeed, there are certain situations in the leadership process, where the preferred method might be less beneficial. In this context, it is essential to learn, differentiate, and identify a preferred style and to learn to use different techniques as needed.

CHAPTER TEN

Employee Co-Leading

The purpose of this chapter is to put another dimension to leadership. Every company has so many challenges to face, as this book describes; therefore, we need to look for solutions that haven't been discussed so much in the rich selection of literature on the market. In this field, we find the employee co-leading. A question is raised in the (my) mind why employee co-leading situations should appear in the first place. Leaders may have concerns over it and ask themselves, "Aren't I the leader?" The employees may have issues over it and say, "Am I employed to lead!" Those with open minds will most potentially be preferred to explore several problems associated with employee co-leading before passing any final judgments. Let's take a brief look into the employee co-leading situation and what it could be like. In my opinion, there are four positives associated with this strategy.

Added Value

The unique interaction between leaders and employees cannot but assist in strongly impacting the energy levels of employees; and being a powerfully productive group experience, in a co-leadership situation.

Sharing of Power and Responsibility

The presence of co-leadership between employers and employees indicates the readiness of each of the employees to take their share of responsibility within their group. This type of work modality is chosen in order to organize the administrative procedures of the group better. By its nature, such a sharing of power between co-leading employees renders obsolete the question of personal power and reinforces the internal management of the overall group.

Flexibility

Flexibility takes the readiness and skill of each of the employees into consideration, maintaining their working style as requirements dictate. This, in turn, allows for supporting a blending or meshing of the two synergies, which create a rhythmic balance as well as harmony within a team, project group, or department.

Growth and Learning

The growth and learning involved in employee co-leading lead to strong motivation, and the readiness of each employee to play their part to create and promote a productive learning environment through the give and take of the knowledge. Employees can open themselves up to reveal their weaknesses as well as strengths, with the result that they will tend to be more receptive to learn from others in the group in a non-threatening atmosphere. The outcome is individual growth and development for all --- as far as I can see.

There are advantages and disadvantages to employee co-leadership, of course, which must be evaluated like any other business structure. A mutual effort might be complicated, creating conflicts along the way. But employee co-leadership allows for greater collaboration and synergy --- ripening the opportunities for a more cohesive and supportive workplace culture and environment.

Advantages of Employee Co-leading

Co-leading Provides More Feedback

An employee co-leading structure offers more pairs of eyes that can recognize potential issues, assess circumstances, or offer thoughts.

Logistics Are Improved With a Co-Leading Dynamic

At the point when employees co-lead, the shared duties make the coordination of pushing ahead simpler for the company, because there is generally speaking greater accessibility. Notwithstanding something as straightforward as employee accessibility improves when there is an employee co-leading structure set up. On account of the positional uniformity, progress can be made regardless of whether the leader isn't accessible for reasons unknown.

It Creates Added Diversity Into the Company and Brand

Diversity causes a company to develop also. With various characters, encounters, and points of view accessible inside, there is more chance for development. Although distinctions in style can lead to conflict triggers, on the off chance that they are adequately dealt with, the understanding of conversations, thoughts, and inspirational feedback will, by and large, improve for the employer.

Co-leading Can Grow Company Revenues Quickly

At the point when there are less non-natural squares set up that influence individual occupation execution, employees have more chances to develop. At the point when there are more open doors to professional development set up, the income generated opens doors for the company to grow also. To create these results, employees need to work together in such a way where their contrasts can be used in a complementary manner, bringing about cooperative energy which leads to greater efficiency.

It Flattens Out the Hierarchy of the Organization

At the point when the employees are set up to co-lead, less accentuation is placed on the hierarchy of leadership in the company. When everybody is included and has a chance to be a leader in their own manner, the company benefits since every action of the company is combined and bolstered by every person in the organization --- not just a select few. That implies there are more open doors for self-awareness and inventiveness, as the constrictions of a strict and convoluted hierarchy are effectively diminished.

Disadvantages of Employee Co-Leading

Some Split Responsibility Problems

There are duties in the workplace which generally have more power associated with them than others. Obligations that include the setting of the strategic direction of a specific department, speculation decisions, or picking key representatives for a particular task would probably put one employee in a more authoritative position over another sometimes. That can lead to feelings of jealousy and resentment. Especially if pay levels are equivalent, employees with unequal amounts of authority can definitely lead to more conflict in the work environment.

Decision-Making Processes Could Increase

Leaders who focus on employee co-leading are less agile when it comes time to settle on a prompt choice. In co-leadership situations, it is a common fact that everybody must have the option to give their contribution before a final decision is made. The issue of lengthy times to reach a final decision can be counterbalanced by having characterized obligations, and essential activities sketched out beforehand, yet there will consistently be times when one person may need to make a final choice if consensus is challenging to reach.

It May Create Confusion in the Workplace

It is probably inevitable that at some point, there will be differences of opinion during a project or team assignment. Employees trapped in these contradictions will show decreased efficiency levels until the disputes can be settled. This working arrangement may likewise create two separate plans for the employees to pursue, which might be contrary to one another.

There Are Increased Expenses for the Company

In a co-leading corporate environment, the company will generally compensate every worker with higher salaries. But on the other hand, some in leadership --- especially supervisors and middle management, might have lower wages in general.

It Creates a Strain on Workplace Morale

Employee co-leading connections can become stressed after some time if one employee has a more exceptional range of abilities than another. The compensation levels for all participants may be equivalent, yet the aptitude levels are different. At that point, friction will probably develop in some relationships in the workgroup. When relationships become stressed, then the confidence of every single employee will plunge lower also.

There Can be an Imbalance with the Corporate Vision

Some employees may have varying degrees of commitment to the business than others. That fact alone can create awkwardness inside the co-leading relationship. If this situation occurs, and there are disparate objectives that are being sought after, the equilibrium of the employer will be influenced too. Contradictions happen regularly where people are concerned unless everybody is committed to the same goals and outcomes.

The employee co-leading structure is very interesting and might be something I take a closer look into further ahead. With this chapter in a fresh mind we also need to look at the most productive time and environment.

CHAPTER ELEVEN

Exploring the Most Motivated and Productive Work Environment

In this chapter, we will take a closer look at work productivity, and when and where performance among employees becomes the best. We will dig into the advantages of remote working but also the consequences of it. Let's start with some facts.

Employees who are offered the choice of adaptable working schedules are profiting UK business by taking less leave and working more productively. A survey examined the productivity of 1,500 workers who set their own hours or designed their work area against 500 who didn't. The adaptable workers reviewed said they found work more enjoyable and stimulating than those working a customary "nine-to-five" job schedule.

Seventy-five percent of these workers further said they'd be hesitant to leave their current work environment if another organization didn't permit similar adaptability. "Adaptable working has a colossal number of advantages for representatives and businesses the same," said Olivia Hill, HR-manager official at AAT, which conducted the survey.

It appears leaders are much more willing to permit flexible hours, as long as the appropriate productivity is maintained. It doesn't generally make a difference when and where the work occurs. The most significant thing is reaching goals and targets in terms of productivity.

Another examination discovered that 20 percent of respondents enquired about work environment adaptability on their first team meeting for a project, and four out of 10 respondents said the choice of flexible working hours were offered, albeit 15 percent said it applied only to them[1].

The study mentioned above also found that employees were more interested in the ability to set the hours they work, instead of picking the area they work from. Only one out of five was more interested in determining where they would conduct their work. The fundamental explanation the review's respondents gave for needing flexible work choices was to balance their home and family existence with work environment needs.

Remote Jobs

Giving autonomous employees a chance to pick their areas can lift companies, representatives, and even the economy. Employers who choose where and when to perform their responsibilities escalate representative productivity, diminish turnover, and lower hierarchical expenses.

While advanced innovation has made employees more productive and open than at any time in recent memory, numerous companies have been slow to give their staff a chance to telecommute consistently --- let alone to work from anyplace whenever. The option to allow employees to work from home would have significant ramifications, allowing workers to live in places that are within their budget --- as opposed to living close to the job to reduce commute times. If allowed to work remotely, then employees can decrease driving expenses, spend less on clothing and food, and live nearer to family and companions.

Work from Anywhere Isn't Feasible for Everyone

For many employers, remote work is a win-win situation because the employee can have more autonomy, and the business will generally see higher productivity and lower staff turnover. Employees with occupations that require insignificant coordination could be eligible for a work-from-home position.

At the point where the virtualizing of work (whenever) and the Data Anywhere development (anyplace) consolidate, they obliterate most existing job conditions. The mindset that all employees go to a specific spot for a set time to perform their assignments is rapidly disintegrating. Since the mentality of younger workers looks for more freedom and versatility, company leaders should consider allowing work to be performed at any time and in any place --- as long as quotas and performance standards can be maintained.

The ascent of anyplace/whenever work can be terrifying. As any leader will be sure to let you know, employees setting their own hours can be a mixed blessing. The lines between work and personal life can blur to the point where the work never stops. Simultaneously, anyplace/whenever working environments will liberate both employers and employees from the chains of outdated work setups to creating company cultures and work environments that genuinely connect with and enhance people.

Why Working Is Beneficial in Offices

Earning a profit takes place when there is a higher consumption of goods and services than there are costs to produce those goods and services Productivity entails getting as much as possible achieved in as little time as possible. Many employers are aware of the advantages of having more productive employees. Productivity advantages are apparent and broadly assumed when integrated into a business atmosphere.

Productivity also identifies how efficiently employees achieve the company's objectives and produce according to the company's mission. By understanding typical reasons for low work efficiency, employers can coach their employees on work ethics, streamlining procedures, and cultivating higher trust among the workforce.

Why Remote Jobs Are Beneficial

Recent studies demonstrate that 70% of individuals work remotely at least once per week. Numerous employers support and encourage remote work. Flexible arrangements allow employees to feel most productive to the company and lets employers procure the most ideally equipped staff for the activity without having to spend a lot of energy on the physical configuration of the office. Cost investment funds are additionally a factor: Dell reports saving about $12 million every year in land costs by urging employees to telecommute.

While remote work offers many advantages, a few companies still prefer for workers to be onsite. IBM, an early adopter of remote work, turned around its arrangement in 2017 by placing many employees back into the workplace, due to the belief that groups working together in the same physical space to be more fruitful. Google discourages working from home on the premise that shared experiences between partners improve overall execution.

Remote-work approaches are prevalent with a lot of employees who point to an improved work-life balance for employees among its advantages. Yet, different employers think employees perform better when they're in the workplace, while representatives who work entirely remotely will, in general, feel secluded.

It is incumbent upon each employer to choose what works best for them, and --- as with most things --- allowing for more than one option might be vital. For example, restricting the quantity of days employees can telecommute will help encourage more face-to-face cooperation. But providing the choice of remote work can be a positive differentiator for leaders looking to set themselves apart from competitors in the work market and pull in top ability from anyplace.

Why Workers Are Looking for Remote Jobs

Work-Life Balance

A strong work ethic doesn't characterize millennials as much as it does for those in previous generations. Doolittle says items like family, companions, and having effects in their social networks are more vital to millennials than they are for older workers. Given this, requests from millennials to set their own work schedules will undoubtedly increase in the future as they offset work responsibilities with bringing up small kids.

What's more, as a growing number of people who were born in the decade and a half after the end of World War II reach retirement age, younger workers will also be drawn to the needs of their aging parents and grandparents. The tradeoff of staying in contact with a colleague by an email at 10 PM, or setting aside a few minutes on a Saturday morning to complete a task --- as far as I can tell --- is a small compromise that millennials are willing to accept.

Continuing Skills Education

Fifty percent of millennials want their leaders to provide training and mentoring to enhance their professional development. Employers who are willing to allow younger workers this "experience-jumping" through in-house training programs that this enables them to test out various new strategies and allocations of duties for the benefit of the organization. The eminent General Electric professional development program is an extraordinary model, which enables youthful employees to encounter different aspects on the inside of GE --- for example, funds, sales, assembling, and building.

Regardless, millennials will invest energy in taking classes and even pursuing additional sources of income to grow their aptitudes and skillsets. Thus, a portion of this pursuit of more experiences and skills will undoubtedly pay off during the typical workday.

The Disappearing Corporate Office

By 2030, experts predict that a majority of the workforce will generally operate from home using quick information terminals. Most employers will have eliminated their remaining physical office areas for chains of interconnected center points with various designs for people to access space. Gatherings will routinely happen virtually, rendering air travel for business meetings superfluous.

The Bottom Line

Millennials want flexible work hours, and this trend should prove beneficial for employers and employees alike. Research by Stanford professor Nicholas Bloom found that working remotely builds productivity, lessens work hours, and enhances worker fulfillment.

Over a nine-month time frame, Bloom watched 250 workers at Ctrip, a Chinese travel site. Half of the employees telecommuted, and the other half worked in the workplace. It turned out, taking into account the time it takes to get to work physically, and the interruptions of the in-office condition had an immense effect: The remote workers completed 13.5% more calls than the employees in the workplace, and also performed 10% more work overall[1].

The Disadvantages of Remote Jobs

So far, we have mostly talked about the benefits of remote jobs. But are there any disadvantages? If so, what are they? I will mention some of them below.

Too Much Work

There is a peril that employees will work too much due to a blurring of boundaries between work and home life. This can result in burnout or other stress-related symptoms if it happens often enough.

Reduced Connection

For an extroverted person, working alone may not be the best choice. Interacting with colleagues by email, phone, instant messaging, or video conferencing could ease the feelings of boredom and isolation. Working from a library or a public space, such as a coffee shop, will help remote workers in their need to meet others. Splitting time between working in the office and at home may help in achieving the benefits of working in an office environment.

Distractions

While employees won't have the traditional work diversions, they need to have good self-control so that they do not spend too much time catching up on TV, cooking, etc. It may be hard sometimes to focus on the job at hand when one's private life is right outside the door. There may be a need for dedicated office space in the home with inhibited diversions and temptations to make it work.

Not Having Full Access to Technology Platforms

Generally, cloud innovation has made it simpler than at any time in recent memory for telecommuters to work from anyplace. Nonetheless, there are circumstances in which information security or purchaser assurance concerns may keep remote workers from having full access to vital data for their work.

Limited Advancement

Working out of the office can make it harder for those employees to stay in the loop. Not being physically present can make it harder to advance through the company and receive promotions. For remote workers, it is crucial to keep up contact with colleagues and management regularly.

Not for Everyone

Not every worker or job is appropriate for working out of the workplace. But those not selected for telecommuting may become discouraged and disenchanted, leading to some staff turnover.

What Is the Future?

As individual companies embrace more extensive work from home approaches, others --- for example, Yahoo! --- have openly withdrawn from enabling workers to venture outside of base camp. Companies have referred to the requirement for office "acknowledgment" and the advantages of unconstrained collaboration among the motivations to maintain a strategic distance from offering remote work --- even to the most profoundly talented, independent employees.

It's a matter of trust, and I believe it's the absence of openness between employers and employees evidenced by the academic research that remain obstacles to more employees working from home. Giving employees, especially those who work independently, the opportunity to choose where and how to perform their jobs could profit employees as well as employers. Employees will then have choices in where they want to live. This was one of the promises of digital innovation --- that technology would enable employees to move away from congested urban centers.
In any case, better productivity --- like other areas in life --- requires some work on employees' end. It can take as long as a quarter of a year to form new habits, regardless of whether that includes making a daily to-do list or working out regularly at the rec center.

When something turns into a habit, it becomes a lot simpler to incorporate into daily practice. By transforming productivity into a pattern, employees can accomplish unmistakably more in their work and their personal life.

Employees would prefer to produce with less exertion. Be that as it may, how might employers compute productivity, not to mention to increment it upward? The initial step is to discover a few models of what enhanced productivity implies and what it doesn't.

Employers' drive to expand productivity starts at work. They should model after a partner noted for their productivity. Search for talents who have a clear goal for each workday sets restraints on their time and even strives to complete tasks early.

By discovering employees that exemplify the sort of significant productivity that impacts those around them in the company, employers can begin to picture what expanding productivity will mean in the future.

CONCLUSION

Throughout this book, we have tried to provide a snapshot of sorts to the future for the corporate world; so that those in leadership would have some ideas to spark further study and discussion. We have also provided some tools to those who wish to pursue some of the key strategies to deal with the challenges in the workforce and economy going forward. To succeed in this economy in the 21st Century, corporate leaders must be able to clearly assess where their company is at, and make the adjustments needed for further growth and vitality.

One of the factors we have stressed in this book is the fact that the workforce itself has changed in the last years, and that younger generations have many different attitudes about work and the workplace than their elders. These differences must be taken into account when shaping a company to be competitive and successful in this changing world. Many of these generational differences can be mitigated, however, by applying some (or all) of the suggestions and ideas presented here.

We spent a lot of content going over the importance of prioritizing building up and empowering the employees. Businesses can no longer rest on past accomplishments and reputation --- except as a foundation to build upon for the future. What will set one company apart from others in their market will be the quality of their workforce, and the passion and energy they provide that makes a positive impact on both their customer base, as well as the talent pool which provides workers for that market.

A company culture that emphasizes an atmosphere of cooperation and collaboration between management and staff, and allows the team to be a part of decisions and setting goals makes itself a magnet for those workers who have the highest skills and the ambition and drive that keeps companies on the cutting edge. Once a vibrant culture is established, it will serve as the best advertising for acquiring the best available employees. And this, in turn, creates a synergy to accentuate the company brand for both potential employees as well as the client/customer base.

Besides having an energetic and positive culture, there are definite factors that a business can put into practice to make sure that new workers who contact the company for open positions will have the qualities and characteristics needed to fit into the culture. We looked at items like networking, the use of social media such as LinkedIn, recruiters, and even the often overlooked avenue of seeking referrals from the current workforce for new workers.

Included in the overall scenario of acquiring and keeping talent is the value of a well-thought-out onboarding process. Citing several documented studies, we demonstrated the importance of a robust onboarding process and described what the significant pieces of an effective onboarding strategy are.

As part of our overview of how to entice the best brightest to join the company staff, we dealt at length with the consideration of designing benefit packages that will be seen as an inviting aspect for gaining new employees --- while at the same time also keeping and rewarding the valuable staff that is already a part of the business. But we also attempted to encourage company leaders to be aware of the growth of the gig economy and to realize that there are several advantages to having at least a portion of the workforce designated as freelancers or contract workers. But the issues already discussed the kind of workers companies want to bring into the company still applies the same to these non-traditional workers.

We then turned our attention to the concept of gamification and the value that can be derived from incorporating this modality as part of the workflow process. Gamification --- when properly applied --- optimizes workflow and keeps workers much more engaged and motivated. This is especially important as the younger generations are so acclimated to gamification as a lifestyle, so why not incorporate its positive aspects into the workplace?

In the latter portions of the book, we delved deeply into different strategies that companies who wish to remain competitive will want to consider and reinforce. Thus, we examined the importance of setting up successes and growth for employees to both maximize the skills and aptitudes of staff, while reducing stress and turnover. This can be accomplished through building trust and responsibility, developing leaders from within through coaching, and acceptance of allowing for open communication and sharing of responsibilities between management and staff.

By implementing such factors as focusing on a vibrant company culture, looking at employees with a greater appreciation of the assets they are for a company, and how to create an environment that helps to attract and keep the best assets --- employees --- companies will be poised to excel in the competitive and dynamic economy that is a fact of life today. Through gamification, employee co-leading, and coaching leaders, businesses can set themselves up for more success and maintain an edge over their competitors.

Our hope is that this book has stimulated some thinking and planning ahead that will show benefits in the long term for companies and leaders who are willing to place themselves under the microscope. Hopefully they will see what the real picture of their company is like today, and then use the ideas presented in this book to make the appropriate adjustments and changes for continued success in the future. No one can predict the future with 100 percent certainty. Still, by drawing on the expertise of others who have done their homework, we have pointed the way to some probabilities of what the workplace and workforce will most likely become in the years ahead. One of our goals has been to assist corporate leaders to be aware of coming changes ahead of time and also to be familiar with some concepts that might sound new today, but we believe they will become the standard in the not-too-distant future. The future is already here in many working sectors.

I believe the hallmark of good leadership is the ability to honestly assess the current status of their business and their market, and then have the willingness to broaden their thinking and take the necessary risks to ensure the future growth and vitality of their business better. The years ahead can be filled with dread or with hope for the economy and overall success of companies--- hopefully, this book will make that bright future easier to envision as some of the ideas presented here are examined and considered.

BIBLIOGRAPHY

[1] How To Build A Positive Company Culture. (2019). Forbes.com. Retrieved 17 August 2019, from
https://www.forbes.com/sites/alankohll/2018/08/14/how-to-build-a-positive-company-culture/#493e3cd949b5

[2] Three company culture challenges – and how to combat them. (2019). Hcamag.com. Retrieved 17 August 2019, from
https://www.hcamag.com/au/news/general/three-company-culture-challenges-and-how-to-combat-them/141640

[3] A Good Way to Change a Corporate Culture. (2009). Harvard Business Review. Retrieved 17 August 2019, from
https://hbr.org/2009/06/the-best-way-to-change-a-corpo

[4] Beamery. (2019). Beamery.com. Retrieved 17 August 2019, from
https://beamery.com/blog/employer-branding

[5] What is Employee Branding? And Why Does Your Company Need It? | ReviewTrackers. (2018). ReviewTrackers. Retrieved 17 August 2019, from https://www.reviewtrackers.com/employee-branding/

[6] What Science Says About Identifying High-Potential Employees. (2017). Harvard Business Review. Retrieved 17 August 2019, from
https://hbr.org/2017/10/what-science-says-about-identifying-high-potential-employees

[7] Attracting and retaining the right talent. (2019). McKinsey & Company. Retrieved 29 August 2019, from https://www.mckinsey.com/business-functions/organization/our-insights/attracting-and-retaining-the-right-talent

[8] 6 Things Wise Leaders Do To Engage Their Employees. (2019). Forbes.com. Retrieved 30 August 2019, from
https://www.forbes.com/sites/glennllopis/2015/02/02/6-things-wise-leaders-do-to-engage-their-employees/#1d1a15577f5d

[9] What Science Says About Identifying High-Potential Employees. (2017). Harvard Business Review. Retrieved 17 August 2019, from

https://hbr.org/2017/10/what-science-says-about-identifying-high-potential-employees

[10] Technology Can Save Onboarding from Itself. (2015). Harvard Business Review. Retrieved 31 August 2019, from https://hbr.org/2015/03/technology-can-save-onboarding-from-itself

[11] Get Your New Managers Moving. (2008). Harvard Business Review. Retrieved 31 August 2019, from https://hbr.org/2008/02/get-your-new-managers-moving-1

[12] New Research on Onboarding and Employee Success. (2016). Cognology. Retrieved 31 August 2019, from https://www.cognology.com.au/new-research-on-onboarding-and-employee-success/

[13] 6 Checklists to Perfect your New Employee Onboarding Process | Process Street | Checklist, Workflow, and SOP Software. (2018). Process Street. Retrieved 31 August 2019, from https://www.process.st/new-employee-onboarding-process/

[14] Five Onboarding Best Practices New Hires Will Thank You For | SmartRecruiters. (2019). SmartRecruiters Blog. Retrieved 31 August 2019, from https://www.smartrecruiters.com/blog/new-employee-onboarding-best-practices/

[15] gig Economy: Definition and Pros and Cons. (2019). ThoughtCo. Retrieved 2 September 2019, from https://www.thoughtco.com/gig economy-4588490

[16] Same reference as in reference number 15

[17] 4 Reasons Why The gig Economy Will Only Keep Growing In Numbers. (2019). Forbes.com. Retrieved 2 September 2019, from https://www.forbes.com/sites/abdullahimuhammed/2018/06/28/4-reasons-why-the-gig economy-will-only-keep-growing-in-numbers/#8e44fb411ebc

[18] (2019). Shrm.org. Retrieved 8 September 2019, from https://www.shrm.org/hr-today/trends-and-forecasting/research-and-surveys/Documents/2015-Job-Satisfaction-and-Engagement-Report.pdf

[19] Nelson, A., & Nelson, A. (2016). Gamification: Playing Your Way to Better Employee Engagement | Hppy. Hppy. Retrieved 9 September 2019, from https://gethppy.com/talent-management/gamification-better-employee-engagement

[20] Gamification to Increase Employee Motivation and Engagement. (2017). Linkedin.com. Retrieved 9 September 2019, from https://www.linkedin.com/pulse/gamification-increase-employee-motivation-engagement-morrison-fcipd

[21] How Gamification in the Workplace Impacts Employee Productivity. (2018). Medium. Retrieved 9 September 2019, from https://medium.com/swlh/how-gamification-in-the-workplace-impacts-employee-productivity-a4e8add048e6

[22] WHY EMPLOYEES NEED FLEXIBILITY. (2019). Workplaceflexibility.bc.edu. Retrieved 10 September 2019, from http://workplaceflexibility.bc.edu/need/need_employees

[23] The Importance of Achieving Work-Life Balance and How To Do It. (2019). The Balance Careers. Retrieved 10 September 2019, from https://www.thebalancecareers.com/work-life-balance-1918292

[24] Why Trust Matters at Work. (2018). SHRM. Retrieved 11 September 2019, from https://www.shrm.org/hr-today/news/hr-magazine/0618/pages/why-trust-matters-at-work.aspx

[25] Bean, S. (2017). Employees with higher levels of trust and autonomy at work are more productive - Workplace Insight. Workplace Insight. Retrieved 11 September 2019, from https://workplaceinsight.net/employees-given-higher-levels-of-trust-and-autonomy-in-the-workplace-increase-performance/

Printed in Dunstable, United Kingdom

91228670R00078